Zacharias Tanee Fomum

ENJOYING THE MARRIED LIFE

Éditions du Livre Chrétien
4, rue du Révérend Père Cloarec
92400 Courbevoie France
editionlivrechretien@gmail.com

First Edition. 1988, 7500 Copies

© Zacharias Tanee Fomum, 1985

Printed by:
Editions du livre chrétien
4, rue du Révérend Père Cloarec
92400 Courbevoie - FRANCE
Tel: (33) 9 52 29 27 72
Email: editionlivrechretien@gmail.com

Covert by:
Jacques Maré

I dedicate this book to

Céline Bidja

Helen Ngankwe

Jacques Yougang

all of them servants of the Lord Jesus

and Faithful co-workers with me in the "Book Ministry"

In grateful acknowledgement of their sacrificial labours

behind the scenes

TABLE OF CONTENTS

Foreword

Marriage was meant to be a wonderful experience. It was meant to be a kind of "heaven on earth." However, for many people it has turned out to be "hell on earth." We believe that the good marriages can be made better and the bad ones made good. That is what this book is about. In it, you will discover how to "ENJOY THE MARRIED LIFE." There are a number of factors that contribute to making the married life enjoyable. We have discussed these factors. They include:

1 - The fundamental problem and the lasting solution.

2 - Sexual matters.

3 - Money matters.

4 - Children in marriage.

5 - Servants in the marriage home.

6 - Relatives and the married life, and other topics.

The topics discussed in this book make it important for

husbands and wives

children and servants

relatives and everybody.

It is also good reading for those who intend to be married some day. It is an ideal gift to your parents, children, servants, relatives and friends.

ENJOYING THE MARRIED LIFE is the third book in the series, "GOD, SEX AND YOU." The books in this series which have already been produced are:

BOOK 1 : Enjoying The Premarital Life.

BOOK 2 : Enjoying the Choice of Your Marriage Partner.

BOOK 3 : Enjoying the Married Life.

BOOK 4 : Divorce and Remarriage.

BOOK 5 : A Successful Marriage: The Husband's Making.

BOOK 6 : A Successful Marriage: The Wife's Making.

The next book in this series, which we shall be publishing very soon, is entitled

BOOK 7 : Solutions To Sexual Problems

BOOK 8 : Solutions To Marital Problems

Make up your mind to read all the books in this series.

If you have been blessed, encouraged, provoked, insulted or angered by this book, please write and share your reaction with me. I am waiting to hear from you.

We send this book out with prayer that it should bring joy, happiness and fulfilment to you, both in this life and in the one hereafter.

YAOUNDE, MARCH 1985

Zacharias Tanee FOMUM

P.O. Box 6090

YAOUNDE - CAMEROON

CHAPTER 1

HOME
THE SWEETEST PLACE
ON EARTH :

The heaven on earth !

There are many difficulties in the world. There are heartaches and much insecurity. Many people are unhappy. However, many people look towards the marriage home as the sweetest place on earth. I talked to a University student. She was 24 years old and in her last term of school. She was all smiles. I asked her what was in the future. This is what she said to me :

"I am in love. I shall soon be married to the one man I love with every cell in my body. He is everything to me. He is so far above all the other men in the world that there is no comparison whatsoever. Yes, we shall soon be married. I shall give all of myself to him and he will have all that I have. All my thoughts, dreams, wishes, yes, all will be his. I shall hold nothing back from him. I shall pour out all of myself on him. I shall love him more with each passing day. He will be my lord, my king, my master. I shall render him instant obedience. I shall rest in his arms. That will be my real home - the security of his arms. I shall rest my head on his chest - that will be my pillow. I shall tell him everything. I shall know his every thought. I shall know his unspoken thoughts. I shall be lost in serving him. He will make me his queen, treat me as his queen and lead me into limitless fulfilment. I shall be happy. I shall be fulfilled. I am counting the days that separate me from that day when I shall be his in every way."

Another student said to me, "I have used many girls. I have never loved any. Why should I have loved them? There was only passion between us. However, I shall soon be married. I have at last found the one with whom I want to settle in life. She is from the village. She attended the village primary school. She is young and fresh. She is innocent and undefiled. She will soon be mine. The bride price has been paid. In the near future, she will be mine. When she comes to me, I shall stop running after all these other women. I shall be faithful to her. I shall supply her needs – all of them. I shall make her happy. We shall have children together. Some will look like me and others will look like her. There will be no quarrels in our home. I shall be kind and she will be obedient. I look forward to it. May that day come quickly!"

Another young man said to me, "Mine will be a home filled with love. My wife will be the queen of our palace and I shall be the king. Our children will be there to make it wonderful. All those who serve us will be treated with respect and dignity. We shall not allow any sharp word to leave our mouths.

We shall allow love to flow with each glance. We shall keep together. We shall eat, play, work, study, etc., together. We shall each contribute to the growth of the other party. We shall set good examples for our children to copy. We shall keep our home sparkling clean and orderly. Everything shall be put in its place. Poor people will be welcome to our table. We shall respect the elderly. Our neighbours will be converted into our friends. We shall not be rich, but we shall have enough to live on. That is the home I am looking forward to having - a home that will be the sweetest place on earth. I shall run to that home when the storms of life assail me and I shall be received there in a warm, loving and unselfish way."

These expectations have been fulfilled in some lives. One man, after having been married for ten years, said, "My wife has been God's greatest gift to me, next only to the gift of eternal life in Jesus Christ. Before she came into my life, I was lonely and unhappy. She brought joy and sunshine to me, and I have lived in it ever since. Before she came into my life, I was a selfish and self-centred young fool, but her love and unselfishness brought

healing and liberation to me; and I am grateful to the Lord for
it. She is just a blessing. Each time I am away from home, I think
of her and miss her and long to be back with her. I do everything
to be back with her. It is always a joy to be back with her, in her
arms and in her embraces; in her love and in her care. We do not
have many material things. The truth is that I do not miss them.
If I were shut up with her in a prison cell with nothing else except each other and our Lord Jesus, I should be perfectly satisfied and want nothing more."

A woman said to me, "I just love my husband. To me he is
better than all the men of the world put together. He is just
above all of them. He is kind and gentle. He is very understanding. I am very clumsy and disorganised, but he patiently puts
my disorder into order, and over the years I am learning to be
orderly. He is a wonderful father to the children. He loves them
and supplies their every need. He carries them in his heart, and
oh! How he prays for them! As a family we know happiness. Our
love is increasing. My heart still misses beats as I wait for him to
come back from work. Some women say that their husbands'
touches do not excite them as they did before. For me, it is just
the opposite. His touches set my whole being on fire now as they
never did before. I am becoming more and more in love with
him. It is as if I were intoxicated with his love, and the intoxi-
cation is only increasing. Where shall it end? I am a blessed woman. I wish many women would know even 10% of the joy that
I am experiencing. To me, heaven has already begun. When Jesus comes, I shall just continue to be in heaven in His immediate
presence, and my joy will continue and be full."

He was thirty-five years old when he saw a book written on
"love in the married life." He said, "I do not need to read that

book. I saw the real thing lived out in the life of my parents. They had very little formal education and so theirs was not something learned from Shakespearean books or the other books. It was a natural love - deep and very beautiful. They were in love from the time I could first recognise love, and they were still in love thirty years afterwards. My father loved my mother fiercely, protectively and passionately. He always said that she was a most special woman. He gave her many sweet names. He was a busy man who was away from home for about 75% of the time, but he wrote back to her almost everyday, and most of the time he sent her a gift. She, on her part, lived at home in expectation of his return. He was an organised and very tidy man and she spent the time making the home spotlessly clean and orderly. She would dress the house with palm fronds and the road leading home with palm fronds. She put her whole self into the preparation for his arrival from his many tours, and I had to help her with some of that work. You could sense that she was preparing for the return of a king. And I think it was; for he was like her king in many ways. Many of his tours were done on foot. I will never forget that day when she and I had to walk for five kilometres in an evening in order to meet him on the way and bring him back. This was when they had been married for 22 years. The flame was burning. When he was at home, he played and joked with her. If they ever quarrelled, I do not know, but I never saw him frown at her. He loved to have her sit by his side and he delighted to hold her hand. When she was returning from the market or from the farm, he would spot her at a distance, immediately stop all that he was doing and go out to welcome her with outstretched arms and smiles; and then he would take her load and walk with her to the house, hand in hand when possible. The whole village talked about their love. It was something from another world that shone on their horizon. Many years after they have been gone, those who knew them have not ceased to talk of those two lovers. Their home was sweet. It was the sweetest place on earth for them. I was born and brought up in that love nest and it is one of the greatest assets of my life. I am not too interested in books about love. I have seen the real thing in real life. My only anxiety is to see it in my own marriage."

CHAPTER 2

HOME :
HELL ON EARTH !

Unlike the stories which have been shared with you in the preceding chapter, I have encountered many people, most of whom have come to me for counsel about their plight in marriage. To them, marriage and the home were not wonderful. They were nightmares, tragedies, heart-ache and heart-break. Some of the people said the following:

"I was thirteen when I was forced to marry a man. He was many years older than I and very experienced in life. He made me more or less into his servant or slave. I did everything for him and he did nothing for me. I did not mind doing things for him because I grew very fond of him. But my problem was his other women. He was so disrespectful and so committed to hurting me that he would sometimes bring a prostitute home, get me out of our bedroom, lock me up in the adjacent room and spend the night with the prostitute on our bed!"

"We were students together at the University. I was proud and quite confident. I had many admirers. Then he came along and started pleading with me to love him and marry him. Although he was good to look at, I was not too impressed. But he continued and, finally, I said, 'Yes,' to him. He continued to be the one who ran after me and flattered me with much attention. In fact, he literally worshipped me. I could get him to do anything for me. It made me feel like a queen. I accepted to marry him. I thought I would be treated in the same way all my life. But I was in for a shock! Things changed after marriage. He did not seem to care anymore. He could now afford to be rude. He began to criticise my manners, my looks, my character, my everything. I could not understand it at all. We had a joint account and all my money went into it. He alone could withdraw money out of the account. He gave me no money. He went away at weekends with his women at my expense. Sometimes, he would mockingly say, "Have a good time. Bye. I am gone," and indeed he would be gone. My whole being was breaking. I felt humiliated and asked myself a million times, 'Is this me or someone else?' Sometimes, it was so horrible that I thought it was a dream from which I would soon wake up; but alas, it is not a dream or it is a dream that has been going on for ten years!"

"I cannot tell precisely how she came into my life, but I think I met her as all the others whom I used for kicks. I had decided that no woman would stick to me. I had read a book: 'How to avoid Matrimony,' and mastered its contents and was faithfully applying them. But this one gave an excuse for not going away from my house the next day. She washed all my clothes, cleaned everything and was very nice. I enjoyed it and said to myself, 'It's not bad, but tomorrow she must go. That is what the rules say.' Before I woke up the next day, she had tidied the house, washed everything, prepared an excellent breakfast and then she woke me up gently, saying, 'Darling, get up and prepare for work.' That day, as I was going to work, I said to myself, 'If I were the marrying type, I would marry this one, but I am not that type. Many of my friends who get married seem to go for the wrong ones who are lazy, rude and so forth. Why do they not look for the right ones? Anyway, this evening is the very last that I will see of her and I must not yield to such weakness. She may be playing a game. Women are unknowable.' The next morning the same thing happened again until five years rolled by quickly and I had two children with her. I then had to face the facts. I reasoned that she had been very good all these five years. She had got my hot water and breakfast ready before waking me up every day. She had tidied the house and was very good to the children.

It would be to my advantage if she stayed and it would do her all the good in the world. I decided to marry her and it was like a dream come true for her. We arranged everything and got married. The day after the marriage ceremony, I woke up. It was five minutes past seven o'clock. She was still lying down by my side. I thought she had overslept, so I hurriedly woke her up and said, 'Please you have overslept. Wake up quickly. I want to go and see someone at once. Let me have hot water for my bath and breakfast in a matter of minutes. Please hurry.' Then I had the shock of my life. She pulled the blanket and covered herself lazily and said to me, 'If you cannot make hot water for yourself, and if you cannot prepare breakfast, you can go without them. And you had better employ a servant to work in the house and a baby nurse to take care of your children. I have been your slave for the last five years. I had always wanted to be married and to have legitimate children. I decided that I would have both at any cost. I paid the price for five years. Yesterday we were legally married. I have got what I wanted. What must I work for now? I need to be taken care of. You, too, should boil water for me and make breakfast for me before I wake up. As you are too full of yourself to do these things, you must pay someone to do them, and please do it as soon as possible, for I am tired, very tired.'"

Apart from these true stories, are those happening in our nation very regularly; and the same things are happening in other countries. You know of the woman who was married to the senior banker and who later on "fell in love" with a sergeant. You must have read how she welcomed her husband home, fed him, gave herself to him and, while he slept, she and three other fellows killed him and bundled the corpse into her blanket. She drove the car to the Sanaga river where they tied him to a stone and dropped him into the river, and then planned to carry out their love affair in what they thought would be a bright future. But the forces of the law stepped in and the culprits were brought to justice. What type of marriage was she involved in? It was for the husband hell on earth and for her, too, it became hell, and what of the memory that their three children will have to live with?

The wife of one of the nation's leading statesmen confessed that her marriage has been decades of hell on earth, and she knows what she is talking about.

Another woman, a financial executive, young and beautiful, with polished manners told me after our third interview, "My husband left me for another woman. I still love him very desperately. It is as if I will go mad one of these days. Why does death not come to me? Each day the children ask, 'When is Daddy coming? We want to see Daddy.' I have lied and lied to the children in order not to destroy their image of him; for they idolise him, but for how long can I continue to deceive these young ones? My whole being is breaking. My job means nothing to me. My salary means nothing. Oh! How hard life has been! I am just thirty-two. What can the future hold for me?"

Another man said, "My wife ran away. She fell in love with my boss. He gave her a good job and moved her away to the next town. I asked my wife not to go. She said that I could divorce her and that she was prepared to pay the alimony. That is the salary I am having for bringing her from the village where she had no future with her First School Leaving Certificate. I paid for her education. I brought her up at great cost to myself. I thought that she should be well-educated so that the children and all of us might have it easier. I made a mistake. I am reaping the consequences of it. I wish I had listened to my friends. They warned me but I believed her. I believed a woman."

CHAPTER 3

MARRIAGE :
THE PROBLEM
AND THE LASTING
SOLUTION

The problem

There is a serious problem in many marriages. Most are broken. Communication is broken. Love is dead. Bitterness and deception reign. Many people are just trying to patch things up for many reasons, including the loss of face that will come with divorce, the future of the children, the problems that are involved in finding another partner, etc.

The problem is not the man or the woman. The problem is the man and the woman. The problem is that marriage was meant to be a kind of trinity including the Lord God, the man and the woman.

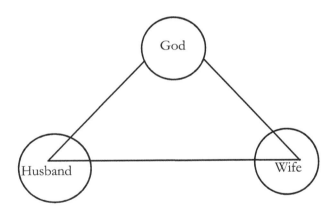

As the husband and wife lived in union with the Lord God, He would establish their love for each other and build them up, solving any problems that would arise between them.

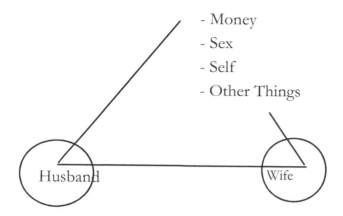

Unfortunately, man sinned, rebelled against God, turned to his own way, and replaced God with a multitude of other things:

money

sex

self

etc.

GOD HAS BEEN REPLACED BY OTHER THINGS THAT CANNOT REALLY HOLD IT TOGETHER. A THREE-LEGGED STOOL HAS LOST ONE OF ITS LEGS, AND WHAT ELSE CAN THERE BE BUT COLLAPSE?

A lasting solution

Because the real problem in marriage is a broken relationship with God, it then manifests itself in selfishness, thoughtlessness and wickedness, whose finished products are :

Pride

Adultery

Anger

Wickedness

Jealousy

Harshness

Laziness, Indiscipline

Gluttony leading to overweight

Drunkenness leading to "pregnant" men

Partiality leading to unfair treatment of the needs of relatives

from the other

family

Dishonesty

Gossip

Slander

Bitterness

Uncleanness

Disorder

An unforgiving attitude

Self-justification

Self-exaltation

Self-condemnation

Degradation of the other partner

Exposure of the weaknesses of the other partner

Ridiculing of the other partner

Ingratitude

Fault-finding, Joylessness, etc.

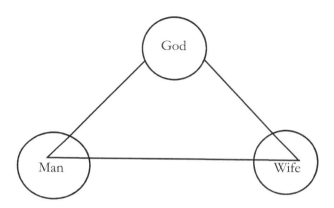

These things are the finished products of a broken relationship with God, and they ruin a marriage. The broken relationship with God has led to a broken or breaking relationship between the two people.

No marriage relationship can satisfy its destiny while the man and woman remain separated from God. There may be some relationship, but it can never be what God meant it to be; for if a car should tell the driver to leave the steering so that it should drive itself, for how long can it stay on the road without causing an accident?

A lasting solution to the marriage problem is by a return to marriage as God meant it to be, with Himself as part of the trinity. This is made possible through the death of Jesus Christ on the cross, that He may bring the sinners back to God and then to Himself and, finally, to each other.

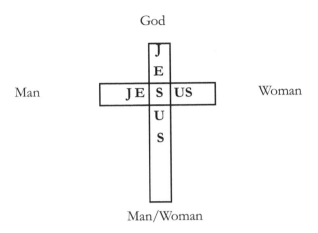

Because of the death of Jesus on the cross, those who turn to Him are brought back to union with God through Him. They are also brought into a proper relationship with each other, and this restores things to what God meant them to be. The roots of selfishness, thoughtlessness and wickedness are broken and, therefore,

pride

adultery

anger

wickedness

jealousy

harshness

laziness

indiscipline

etc..

disappear, giving way to a harmonious relationship that fulfils.

One other thing

God's purpose in marriage was that a man should receive a wife from Him, and that this woman was to help him to accomplish His (God's) work. Can there be real happiness for people who forget what God's original purpose was and make themselves the goal of the marriage relationship?

This is the way to a lasting solution: Repentance towards God followed by faith in the Lord Jesus and a commitment to seeking God's purpose for marriage, and doing it. There is no substitute for this. A change in partners will not do it. God is able to do it. Let Him do it now.

CHAPTER 4

SEXUAL MATTERS
IN MARRIAGE

S ex is an integral part of the married life. God, the Author of marriage, said, *"Therefore a man leaves his father and his mother and cleaves to his wife, and they become one flesh"* (Genesis 2:24). The Bible again says, *"The husband should give to his wife her conjugal rights, and likewise the wife to her husband. For the wife does not rule over her own body, but the husband does; likewise the husband does not rule over his own body, but the wife does. Do not refuse one another except perhaps by agreement for a season, that you may devote yourselves to prayer; but then come together again, lest Satan tempt you through lack of self-control"* (1 Corinthians 7:3-5).

To attempt to minimise the importance of sex in marriage is not right. Sex is very important in marriage. I have counselled many couples and I can honestly say that any marriage that fails in bed is mostly going to fail in an overall sense. The marriage that succeeds in bed has a good chance of overall success. Many married people who have come to my clinic (The clinic for Spiritual, Emotional, Psychological, Marital and Physical Diseases), have said things like the ones below :

1 My wife is cold and unresponsive. I am unsatisfied.

2 My husband is always in a hurry, so much so that when it is over, I am unsatisfied and unfulfilled.

3 My wife is dirty. I dread any contact with her because of the odour that puts me off entirely. I have told her to clean up by bathing each evening, but she does not, yet she expects me to desire her. How can I ?

4 My husband bathes once a week. He does not seem to have the sense of smell. When he approaches me, his odour puts me off. Each relationship with him is an ordeal.

5 My husband shouts at me from dawn do dusk and at night he

expects me to be warm and responsive to him. He does not understand that a good relationship at night is the result of gentleness and kind words from the morning. I am used as a thing and, therefore, I just let him have my body, but I do not give him my real self. How can I give him my true self when I am suffering from the wounds of his hard and harsh words?

6 From the day when my wife told me that she had known many men in the past and committed two abortions, all my interest in her disappeared. She is like my sister and no more. How can I become one of the multitudes of men that she has known? How can I become one with a murderess?

7 My husband is unfaithful. I know the women and girls he runs after. Sometimes I see his letters and they drive me mad. I love him and I hate him. I want to give myself to him, but I also want to hurt him. I am torn inside. I am broken. Can you help me?

8 I married a slim young girl. She weighed 53 kilos then. She was pretty and attractive and I delighted in her. Now after 7 years of marriage, I have a small elephant weighing 82 kilos. When I look at her everything in me dies. All the love I had for her has disappeared. This is not the one I married. I keep blaming myself for having chosen wrongly. She wants me but her size frightens me from inside. Her whole person crushes me. I still long for my girl of 53 kilos.

9 Since I got married, I have known only one man - my husband. My problem is that I have to be treated so often for venereal diseases. My husband is certainly at the root of it. How can I give myself fully to an unfaithful man whose unfaithfulness brings diseases to me?

10 She first came to our home as a sister to my husband's

friend. I took care of her and then I found out that she was having an affair with my husband. At the moment, she is already his wife and they both mistreat me.

11 My wife wants sexual union once a month and I am starving and frustrated.

Many marriages are failing in the sexual realm. These problems can be arranged into four groups:

1 Marital unfaithfulness.

2 Unkind or unloving treatment of each other.

3 Physically unattractive and dirty mates.

4 Incompatibility.

The first two of these problems have a spiritual background and must have spiritual treatment! The next two must have practical treatment.

Marital unfaithfulness

When a man gets married, he ought to stop all other sexual relationships. God expects this from him. He expects the same from his wife. Unfortunately, there are many people who are carrying out extramarital relationships. This is a great sin against God. The Word of God speaks clearly about this. It says, *"Drink water from your own cistern, flowing water from your own well. Should your springs be scattered abroad, streams of water in the streets? Let them be for yourself alone, and not for strangers with you. Let your fountain be blessed, and rejoice in the wife of your youth, a lovely hind, a graceful doe. Let her affection fill you at all times with delight, be infatuated always with her love. Why should you be infatuated, my son, with a loose woman and embrace the bosom of an adventuress? For a man's ways are before the eyes of the Lord, and he watches all his paths. The iniquities of the wicked ensnare him, and he is caught in the toils of his sin. He dies for lack of discipline, and because of his great folly he is lost"* (Proverbs 5:15-23).

"My son, keep your father's commandment, and forsake not your mother's teaching. Bind them upon your heart always; tie them about your neck. When you walk, they will lead you; when you lie down, they will watch over you; and when you awake, they will talk with you. For the commandment is a lamp and the teaching a light, and the reproofs of discipline are the way of life, to preserve you from the evil woman, from the smooth tongue of the adventuress. Do not desire her beauty in your heart, and do not let her capture you with her eyelashes; for a harlot may be hired for a loaf of bread, but an adulteress stalks a man's very life. Can a man carry fire in his bosom and his clothes not be burned? Or can one walk upon hot coals and his feet not be scorched? So is he who goes in to his neighbour's wife; none who touches her will go unpunished. Do not men despise a thief if he steals to satisfy his appetite when he is hungry? And if he is caught, he will pay sevenfold; he will give all the goods of his house. He who commits adultery has no sense; he who does it destroys himself. Wounds and dishonour will he get, and his disgrace will not be wiped away" (Proverbs 6:20-33).

"My son, keep my words and treasure up my commandments with you; keep my commandments and live, keep my teachings as the apple of your eye; bind them on your fingers, write them on the tablet of your heart. Say to wisdom, 'You are my sister,' and call insight your intimate friend; to preserve you from the loose woman, from the adventuress with her smooth words. For at the window of my house I have looked out through my lattice, and I have seen among the simple, I have perceived

among the youths, a young man without sense, passing along the street near her corner, taking the road to her house in the twilight, in the evening, at the time of night and darkness. And lo, a woman meets him, dressed as a harlot, wily of heart. She is loud and wayward, her feet do not stay at home; now in the street, now in the market, and at every corner she lies in wait. She seizes him and kisses him, and with impudent face she says to him: 'I had to offer sacrifices, and today I have paid my vows; so now I have come out to meet you, to seek you eagerly, and I have found you. I have decked my couch with coverings, coloured spreads of Egyptian linen; I have perfumed my bed with myrrh, aloes, and cinnamon. Come, let us take our fill of love till morning; let us delight ourselves with love. For my husband is not at home; he has gone on a long journey; he took a bag of money with him; at full moon he will come home.' With much seductive speech she persuades him; with her smooth talk she compels him. All at once he follows her, as an ox goes to the slaughter, or as a stag is caught fast till an arrow pierces its entrails; as a bird rushes into a snare; he does not know that it will cost him his life. And now, O sons, listen to me, and be attentive to the words of my mouth. Let not your heart turn aside to her ways, do not stray into her paths; for many a victim has she laid low; yea, all her slain are a mighty host. Her house is the way to Sheol, going down to the chambers of death" (Proverbs 7:1-27).

These passages say a lot. Remember what they say of the adulterer or adulteress: "For a man's ways are before the eyes of the Lord, and he watches all his paths."

"So is he who goes in to his neighbour's wife; none who touches her will go unpunished."

"He who commits adultery has no sense; he who does it destroys himself."

"For many a victim has she laid low; yea, all her slain are a mighty host. Her house is the way to Sheol, going down to the chambers of death."

The Bible continues to speak to the adulterer and adulteress, saying,

"Do you not know that the unrighteous will not inherit the kingdom of God? Do not be deceived; neither the immoral, nor idolaters, nor adulterers, nor sexual perverts, nor thieves, nor the greedy, nor drunkards, nor revilers, nor robbers will inherit the kingdom of God" (1 Corinthians 6:9-10).

"Shun immorality. Every other sin which a man commits is outside his body; but the immoral man sins against his own body" (1 Corinthians 6:18).

"Now the works of the flesh are plain: fornication, impurity, licentiousness, idolatry, sorcery, enmity, strife, jealousy, anger, selfishness, dissension, party spirit, envy, drunkenness, carousing, and the like. I warn you, as I warned you before, that those who do such things shall not inherit the kingdom of God" (Galatians 5:19-21).

"But as for the cowardly, the faithless, the polluted, as for murderers, fornicators, sorcerers, idolaters, and all liars, their lot shall be in the lake that burns with fire and sulphur, which is the second death" (Revelation 21:8).

"Blessed are those who wash their robes, that they may have the right to the tree of life and that they may enter the city by the gates. Outside are the dogs and sorcerers and fornicators and murderers and idolaters, and every one who loves and practises falsehood" (Revelation 22:14-15).

God is talking to you adulterer and adulteress.

You may be
    a minister in the government
    a priest
    a pastor
    a secretary-general
    a director
    a chief of service.

You may be
    a university teacher
    a secondary school teacher
    a primary school teacher
    a university or secondary school student.

You may be
    a business man
    a worker in a factory or government
    a farmer
    a jobless person.

You may be
    a professional harlot
    a working class harlot
    a girl in the university

a girl in the secondary school
a jobless girl around town
a village girl.

You may be a rich adulterer or adulteress
a poor adulterer or adulteress
an illiterate adulterer or adulteress
an educated adulterer or adulteress.

You may be in Yaounde, Douala, Bamenda or Garoua.

You may be in Lagos, Accra, Dakar, Nairobi or Kampala.

You may be in London, Paris, Frankfurt or Berlin.

You may be a Communist in Moscow or a Capitalist in Washington.

If you are an adulterer or adulteress, God knows you. You have been caught in the act by Him, even if nobody else saw you. You are guilty before Him, even if you pretend to be guiltless before your wife or husband. There is no place where you can hide and commit adultery without His knowing. You may put out your own lights, but His own lights are always on. You may bolt the door, you may lock it, but it is open to Him. You may be in a hidden hotel or car park or farm. All these places are bare before Him and He is there. He sees all and He records all.

The Bible says, *"A man's ways are before the eyes of the Lord, and he watches all his paths"* (Proverbs 5:21). *"Whither shall I go from thy Spirit? Or whither shall I flee from thy presence? If I ascend to heaven, thou art there!"* (Psalm 139:7-8). Nothing that you have done is hidden from Him. You will stand before Him some day to give account of your ways. The Bible says, *"Then I saw a great white throne and him who sat upon it; from his presence earth and sky fled away, and no place was found for them. And I saw the dead, great and small, standing before the throne, and books were opened. Also another book was opened, which is the book of life. And the dead were judged by what was written in the books, by what they had done. And the sea gave up the dead in it. Death and Hades gave up the dead in them, and all were judged by what they had done. Then Death and Hades were thrown into the lake of fire. This is the second death, the lake of fire; and if any one's name was not found written in the book of life, he was thrown into the lake of fire"* (Revelation 20:11-15).

Dear friend, do you see what it means? The Bible is saying that if you are an adulterer or adulteress, or if you are guilty of any of the other sins that have been spelt out, if you love and practise falsehood and lying in a small way or in a big way; in jokes and the like, you will be thrown into the lake of fire and you will burn there for ever and ever.

Will you not do something about it?

The problem is deeper than the act

The problem is not just the act of a sexual relationship that is forbidden by God. The problem is with man's heart. The Bible says, *"The heart is deceitful above all things, and desperately corrupt; who can understand it?"* (Jeremiah 17:9).

"For from within, out of the heart of man, come evil thoughts, fornication, theft, murder, adultery, coveting, wickedness, deceit, licentiousness, envy, slander, pride, foolishness. All these evil things come from within, and they defile a man" (Mark 7:21-23).

"You have heard that it was said, 'You shall not commit adultery.' But I say to you that every one who looks at a woman lustfully has already committed adultery with her in his heart" (Matthew 5:27-28).

Adultery begins in the heart and ends in the body. The act is the final step in a process that started in the heart. God looks at the heart and not just at the act.

A new heart

Because the problem is with the heart, a lasting solution must include a new heart. Many have tried to solve the problem of adultery in many ways, but no lasting solution is ever attained without a new heart.

God is able to replace the adulterous heart by a new heart. He says in the Bible, *"I will sprinkle clean water upon you, and you shall be clean from all your uncleannesses, and from all your idols I will cleanse you. A new heart I will give you, and a new spirit I will put within you; and I will take out of your flesh the heart of stone and give you a heart of flesh. And I will put my spirit within you, and cause you to walk in my statutes and be careful to observe my ordinances"* (Ezekiel 36:25-27).

The water talks of cleansing. When Jesus died on the cross, He shed His blood for your sin. If you repent of your sin and turn to Him, He will cleanse you of all the sins that you have ever committed.

Then He will take away the old, stony heart with its tendency towards adultery and all the other sins. He will take it away and not leave you without a heart. He will put a new heart within you. This new heart will not be adulterous. It will hate adultery and love righteousness. You will hate adultery and love righteousness.

In addition, He will put His Spirit, the Holy Spirit, within you. The Holy Spirit that He will put within you will enable you to continue to hate sin in all its forms, and He will teach you to love the Lord with all your heart and do what He requires. You will be under new management. Your tendency towards lust, immorality and other sins will be gone and you will find yourself loving the Lord, loving His Word, loving the people who love Him and loving all else that you could not have loved before, because of the new Spirit, the Holy Spirit, that has been put into you.

Will you not receive this new heart now? You can receive it by following the steps below:

Admit that you have personally sinned in your words, thoughts and deeds. Admit that you have committed adultery and/or fornication in your thoughts and (perhaps) in your deeds. Admit to God that you have lusted after beautiful girls in your heart; that you have desired men in your heart and perhaps sinned with them in action.

Admit that you have sinned in other ways, including, perhaps, lying, stealing, anger, theft, wickedness, jealousy, pride, selfishness, etc. Admit that you have committed these sins before God and against God, and acknowledge that they were committed knowingly. Admit that you rightly deserve God's punishment in the lake of fire and sulphur for all that you have done. Admit to God that that is the place of eternal punishment that you deserve.

Believe that when Jesus Christ went to the cross and died there, He took all your sins - past, present and future with Him and crucified them there, washing them away in the blood of His cross. Believe that when He died on the cross, He died where you ought to have died, and that when he died there, you died with Him. Believe that He did that work for the whole world in general and for you in particular. Believe that no one else could have done it and that He is the only way for you out of your mess. Believe that He loves you and is willing to receive you now and give you a new heart and a new spirit. Believe that He will keep you in Himself until the end and that He will not cast you away.

Confess all your sins to Him now and ask Him to take them all away. However, consider the cost of following Him. If He is to forgive you, it will have to be on condition that you are determined to stop sinning. You will, therefore, have to break up with all the sinful relationships that you have been involved in and stop them permanently. You will have to return things that you acquired deceitfully, probably by selling your body or through corruption. You will have to commit yourself to loving Him and serving Him. You will have to study His Word, know it and tell others about Him. You will have to put all that you have and all that you are at His disposal, being prepared to use yourself and all that you have in any way that He may lead you. The supreme goal of your life will have to be to separate yourself unto Him and fully identify yourself with those who love Him and are serving Him. If you are not prepared for these things, or if you are not willing that He should teach you and lead you into them, then you should not bother at all. He will not forgive the sins of those who are half-hearted. He will not forgive those who want to play games with Him. He paid a total price for you on the cross and He will only accept you if you, too, want to come to Him in a total way and on His own conditions. If you are prepared to come on His conditions, then there is something to do.

Pray. Ask Him to come into your life now. Pray a prayer like the following or one of your own: "Lord God, I am a sinner and have sinned in my thoughts, in my words and in my actions. I deserve to be punished now and in eternity because of my sins. Lord, I cannot save myself, but I believe that You sent Jesus Christ to die on the cross for me. I now receive Him, the Saviour Jesus Christ, into my heart and life. Lord Jesus, come into my heart now, wash away all my sin, give me a new heart and a new spirit (Your Holy Spirit) now. Take me. I am Yours now and for ever." Amen.

If you prayed the above prayer in total sincerity, then the Lord has forgiven you, washed away your sin, given you a new heart, put His Holy Spirit within you and made you a child of God.

You are now a child of God. Adultery in all its forms is finished. The problems in your sexual relationship that resulted from marital unfaithfulness have received a permanent solution.

Because you have given your life to the Lord Jesus, the first group of problems (i.e. marital unfaithfulness), is solved permanently for you. If your mate makes the same commitment to the Lord Jesus, then that problem will be solved for him or her too. This will mean that the problem is solved for both of you permanently. Men in whose hearts Jesus lives do not commit adultery. Women in whose hearts Jesus lives do not commit adultery. I insist that when Jesus comes into the lives of both husband and wife, the problem of adultery is solved for the couple permanently. Maybe, you should stop thinking about your mate. You should give your life to the Lord Jesus and He will use you to bring your mate to Him.

The second problem was unkind and unloving treatment of each other. This problem, too, is solved by a commitment to the Lord Jesus. The new spirit that Jesus has given you is actually the Holy Spirit. He is the Spirit of God. When He dwells in a person, He transforms the person completely. He does this by producing His fruit in that person. You may ask what His fruit is.

His fruit has many sides to it. The Bible says, "But the fruit of the Spirit is love,

joy,

peace,

patience,

kindness,

goodness,

faithfulness,

gentleness,

self-control."

As Jesus' people, your lives will manifest these characteristics, and it is obvious that a life that manifests love, joy, patience, etc., cannot be unkind and unloving. You see, the love produced by the Holy Spirit will replace the unloving attitude, while the kindness replaces the unkind attitude. Do you see then that Jesus will solve your problem from its very root? Let me just draw your attention to the fact that you will have all these nine aspects of the fruit of the Holy Spirit from the very moment that you give your life to the Lord Jesus. However, you need time with the Lord Jesus to have the fruit mature and manifest these characteristics to the fullest.

The third problem of a physically unattractive and dirty mate is more of a practical nature, and even here the Lord Jesus provides a solution. If your mate is naturally physically unattractive, you should not blame him or her. You chose him/her. Why did you not look at him or her more carefully? The situation is not hopeless. Pray about it. Ask the Lord to make your mate more attractive. I do not know what He will do, but I do know that He will do something. I know a number of unattractive people whom He has made attractive. Pray to Him. He will show you what you can do to improve your looks. Maybe you need longer hair. Ask Him. He will give you. If you are overweight, you are spoiling your marriage. Ask the Lord to help you to cut down your weight. After all, the Holy Spirit who dwells in you is the Spirit of self-control. Ask Him to help you to control your appetite and so your weight will go down.

The dirty partner should do something about it. If your husband is dirty, tell him. The same thing applies to a dirty wife. Be bold. Tell him or her. "Darling, you need a bath. I will go and get the water ready for you." Speak lovingly and it will communicate. You may have to do this over and over. If your husband is dirty, he has perhaps lived as a dirty man for 20, 25, or 30 years. He is more at home in dirt. It will take time for him to see that his habit is bad and want to change it. The same thing applies to a dirty wife. So, be patient. Continue to encourage your mate. Do everything that is practically possible to help the one who has the problem. Pray about it alone. Pray about it together. Ask the Lord to help you. You see that this is something from the devil to destroy your marriage.

Do not give in.
Do not grumble.
Do not complain.
Do not continue to criticise the faulty person.

These attitudes will not help. They may hinder the person. You should think of ways of encouraging your overweight wife or husband. Maybe you should decide to give a good gift for each kilogram of weight that is lost. Make the promise to her and when she loses the weight, make sure that you give her the thing that was promised.

The fourth problem is that of incompatibility. We already stated in Book Two in this series that there should be sexual compatibility. What if you find that you are sexually incompatible? Your partner may want the sexual relationship more frequently than you, or your partner may be warmer or colder than you in the sexual area of your life together. If this is the case, do not throw away the marriage. Part of the challenge of the married life is that you can adjust to each other. A mature person is prepared to adjust. The best thing to do is first to talk about it very frankly without any hypocrisy. The person who is not satisfied should do so. In my clinic, I have talked to men who were not satisfied. I have also talked to women who would want the relationship more often and who are not fulfilled by the little they are having.

If both of you have given your lives to the Lord Jesus and are, therefore, committed to obeying Him, then it should be easier to solve your problem. The Bible says, "*The husband should give to his wife her conjugal rights, and likewise the wife to her husband. For the wife does not rule over her own body, but the husband does; likewise the husband does not rule over his own body, but the wife does. Do not refuse one another*" (1 Corinthians 7:3-6). The following points come out of this passage :

1. The husband has a right to as much sex as he wants from his wife.

2. The wife has a right to as much sex as she wants from her husband.

3. The partner who is not satisfying the other is the one causing the problem.

4. The partner who is not satisfying the other is the one who has the primary responsibility to improve the situation.

5. Each partner must say, "I have the duty to satisfy my partner. I must do all I can to do so. I have no right to refuse the relationship."

6. The partner who is not responding as much as the other one wants should be seeking ways of improving his/her response in prayer. If the wife is the less responsive, she should pray in the following way, " Lord God, I thank you for the husband you have given to me. I desire to satisfy him completely. Unfortunately, I am not able to do so now. I am rather cold and less responsive. You made my body. You can remake it now. I pray in the name of the Lord Jesus that you should touch my whole being and change it so that I will be as warm and as responsive to my husband as he desires." Of course, if the man is the cold and less responsive partner, he should pray the above prayer. God will answer the prayer and carry out the needed transformation. Is He not the Lord of miracles? Did He not bring the dead back to life? The above prayer can only come from someone who loves the partner and wants to satisfy him or her. It can only come from those who are humble to acknowledge their need. The proud of heart will justify themselves and say, "He is a bother with his demands. Why does he not leave me alone?"

Where such pride exists, the marriage is bound to fail, unless something is done quickly to remedy the situation.

7.   The partner who is not being satisfied should also pray for the other one and ask the Lord for power to wait patiently while the Lord works out the needed transformation in the other party.

8.   Both partners should pray about the problems they have in their sexual life. Sometimes things hidden in the past have to be confessed to each other before harmony is reached in the sexual life. Habits may have to be broken and areas of the personality that are held in bondage may have to be liberated before there is full and satisfying sexual union. Some wives hold grudges against their husbands for things they did or said many years back, perhaps during their courtship days, and such grudges stand in the way of a satisfying sexual relationship for both parties. An unforgiving spirit is a dangerous spirit. It will destroy the person and others. Is that your case? Will you not repent at once and receive forgiveness for your sin? You should.

9.   There are wives who expect their husbands to beg them each time and to run after them. I also hear of husbands who expect their wives to run after them and beg them before there is sexual union. All those who wait to be begged and encouraged are immature. The mature person takes the initiative towards satisfying the other. The mature person does not wait to be begged. He is prepared to beg. If the wife is permanently immature so that she always has to be begged, then she is still a baby. She is not ripe for marriage, even if she is forty years old. To think of a man who is immature to always want his wife to beg him is also to think of a family that is being headed by a

baby. If you are mature, take the initiative. If you are mature, make it your aim to give your partner the greatest pleasure possible. In satisfying your partner you will yourself be satisfied, not only in the sexual area but also in the other areas of the married life. I know of husbands who mistreat their wives because they are not satisfied in their sexual lives. I also know women who are rude and disrespectful to their husbands because the husbands do not satisfy them sexually.

Super sex

The picture that the Bible paints of what should be the sexual life of those who are reconciled to God through the Lord Jesus Christ is that of a relationship which can be called **super sex**. It is something totally satisfying and totally fulfilling.

The Bible says, *"Let your fountain be blessed, and rejoice in the wife of your youth, a lovely hind, a graceful doe. Let her affection fill you at all times with delight, be infatuated always with her love"* (Proverbs 5:18-19).

"You have ravished my heart, my sister, my bride, you have ravished my heart with a glance of your eyes, with one jewel of your necklace. How sweet is your love, my sister, my bride! How much better is your love than wine, and the fragrance of your oils than any spices!" (Song of Solomon 4:9-10).

In the sexual love presented in the Bible, a man said this of his bride: *"How graceful are your feet in sandals, O queenly maiden! Your rounded thighs are like jewels, the works of a master hand. Your navel is a rounded bowl that never lacks mixed wine. Your belly is a heap of wheat, encircled with lilies. Your two breasts are like two fawns, twins of a gazelle. Your neck is like an ivory tower. Your eyes are pools in Heshbon, by the gate of Bathrabbim Your nose is like a tower of Lebanon, overlooking Damascus. Your head crowns you like Carmel, and your flowing locks are like purple; a king is held captive in the tresses. How fair and pleasant you are, O loved one, delectable maiden! You are stately as a palm tree, and your breasts are like its clusters. I say I will climb the palm tree and lay hold of its branches. Oh, may your breasts be like clusters of the vine, and the scent of your breath like apples, and your kisses like the best wine that goes down smoothly, gliding over lips and teeth"* (Song of Solomon 7:1-9).

And the bride said the following of her man, *"My beloved is all radiant and ruddy, distinguished among ten thousand. His head is the finest gold; his locks are wavy, black as a raven. His eyes are like doves beside springs of water, bathed in milk, fitly set. His cheeks are like beds of spices, yielding fragrance. His lips are lilies, distilling liquid myrrh. His arms are rounded gold set with jewels. His body is ivory work, encrusted with sapphires. His legs are alabaster columns, set upon bases of gold. His appearance is like Lebanon, choice as the cedars. His speech is most sweet, and he is altogether desirable. This is my beloved and this is my friend, O daughters of Jerusalem"* (Oh daughters of Cameroon) (Song of Solomon 5:10-16).

The unfaithful wife said to the fool she was trapping, after she had seized and kissed him, *"I had to offer sacrifices, and today I have paid my vows, so now I have come out to meet you, to seek you eagerly, and I have found you. I have decked my couch with coverings, coloured spreads of Egyptian linen; I have perfumed my bed with myrrh, aloes, and cinnamon. Come, let us take our fill of love till morning; let us delight ourselves with love"* (Proverbs 7:13-18).

Why does the wife not do the same to her husband? Why must it be the seducer who puts up an excellent performance? Is that not one reason why they win? Even the most brutal man is tender and soft to a girl he is dating.

He speaks softly to her.

He waits on her.

He is understanding.

He is patient.

He ignores her faults.

He lavishes praises on her.

He does everything to give her all she wants.

He does not shout at her, etc.

Why must the husband not offer this same treatment to his wife and more? It could transform a marriage.

Will you do something about it?

With a new heart from God and the Holy Spirit with you, and Jesus guiding and enabling you, you can do it. God bless you!

CHAPTER 5

MONEY MATTERS IN MARRIAGE

Money matters are a constant source of trouble in many marriages. There are a number of reasons for this. As I have talked with many couples, the problems can be summed up as expressed below:

"My husband is a spendthrift. He can spend a fortune in a day."

" My wife keeps some of the food money for herself and hides behind the fact of inflation."

"My husband is totally selfish. He thinks only of himself. He uses the money on himself and spends nothing on me and the children."

"My wife is very careless. If I give her all at once food money that should last for one month, she will use it in two weeks. That is why I give her the money now on a weekly basis. Maybe some day I will be forced to give it to her on a daily basis."

"My husband gives me food money on a daily basis. This means that I have to go to the market every day and buy things more expensively because I am compelled to buy things at retail prices. If I had money for, say, one month, I could buy a bag of rice and other things in bulk and this would reduce the cost of running the home and save time. But how can I get him to understand?"

"My wife insists that she must have a separate account of her own. She has refused to let us have a joint account. She says that if I am truly a man I should be able to supply all the needs of my home. She often asks why I am interested in her money, asking whether I married her in order to improve my financial situation."

"I made the mistake of my life when I agreed to have a joint account with my husband. How could I be so foolish? He uses my money to rent houses, buy clothes and other things for other women. They are, therefore, well dressed and I am poorly dressed and he prefers them."

"My husband never gives me any pocket money. I have to beg him for every franc. I am treated like a servant or maybe a slave. I have to account for all the money that he gives me right to the last franc. He calculates everything methodically. I think he's got a degree in economics from a Stingy University."

"I am not a fool to tell a woman what I earn. That would be to court disaster. Only fools bring women into their money matters, and such fools do not seem to know that there is the Association of Happy Widows."

"I do not know how much my husband earns. How can I fully stand by him? I do not know if he has a financial strain or not. I only hear him saying that I will cause his bankruptcy. I wish I knew how much he earns. We could plan together. I live in continuous fear and uncertainty. I do not know when I should ask him for a pair of shoes for myself or a dress for our daughter."

"It is a terrible thing to marry these educated girls. They want to know everything. They even want to know how much you are earning, where you are saving, what plot you are planning to buy and what type of house you plan to build. Oh! for those good old days when a man was a man!"

"How can I have the same account with my wife? How can we have property in common? Do you not see that that will complicate things on the day on which we have to be divorced? It will then be difficult to know who had what. To avoid such complications, our marriage is being run under the philosophy, 'Each person for himself and God for us all.' That is safe and reasonable."

"My husband's relatives are taken care of. Nothing is ever done for my own people."

No marriage can be happy when there are financial frictions. Is there a way out of this? Yes, there is. The way out is based on a Christian philosophy for money matters in marriage. This philosophy will work for you as it has worked for multitudes of others who are having no problems whatsoever in their finances as married people.

First of all, realise that you and your partner were not made in the image of money. You will not be satisfied just with money. You were made in the image of God.

For you to have a satisfied financial married life, God must have His rightful place as God in your lives. Although God created man in His image, man sinned and is, therefore, out of deep touch with God. Man is, therefore, running a financial system outside the authority and control of God. Such a godless economic system, even at its very best, must fail. The only way back is for both of you to come back to God, confess to Him that you cannot run your lives and your finances on your own. Tell Him that you have tried to do so but it has not worked. Ask Him to forgive you for your unholy independence from Him all this while. Confess all the other sins in your lives to Him and ask Him to help you. He is willing to accept you and start all over with you. However, you must each come to Him individually. You must come to Him through His Son Jesus Christ, who died on the cross for your sin and rose again from the dead and now lives for ever. When you come to Him through Jesus Christ, He will forgive you, change you and make each one of you into a brand new person. The Bible says, *"Therefore, if any one is in Christ, he is a new creation; the old has passed away, behold, the new has come. All this if from God, who through Christ reconciled us to himself"* (II Corinthians 5:17-18).

Secondly, as people who have received God's love and God's forgiveness, you are to run your financial matters under the full control of Jesus and in total openness to each other. Because you are husband and wife, all that the husband has belongs to both of you and all that the wife has belongs to both of you. You are one. Neither of you should hide any financial matter from the other. No one should use the family income without consulting the other so that both of you are fully agreed on that usage. It does not matter whether one or both of you are working. The income of one person belongs to both of you and the income of both of you belongs to both of you. All the property and funds that the wife had before marriage belong to both of you and all the property and funds that the husband had before marriage belong to both of you.

I suggest the following as a way of running your finances month by month: When your money comes, both of you should take it to your room, kneel down together and thank the Lord who has saved you and who lives in you. He is the One who gave you power to earn that money and so He should be thanked for it. This is a serious matter, for without Him you might have been sick, dead, out of a job, etc., and that would have made it impossible for you to earn the money. The wife should thank the Lord for her husband's capacity to earn money and pray for him and for his job. The husband should thank the Lord for the wife's earning capacity, and pray for her and for her job. If she works in the house, he should thank the Lord for the work she does in the house that contributes to the welfare of the home. Then the wife should thank the man for working and bringing in the money, and the husband should do the same.

The next thing that you should both do is to hold up your money together to the Lord and dedicate it to Him. Ask Him to be Lord of it and to enable you to use it in the way that He wants it used. Ask Him to multiply it and help it to meet all the needs that He wants it to meet. After prayer, sit down and work out a family budget from the joint income of both of you. I suggest that the budget should include the following:

1 A contribution to the work of the Lord.
2 Rent.
3 Food.

4 Savings.

5 Transportation.

6 Water, electricity and gas.

7 Wife's pocket money.

8 Husband's pocket money.

9 Wife's relatives.

10 Husband's relatives.

11 House help.

12 Children's needs.

13 The poor.

14 Entertainment.

15 Unforeseen expenditures.

Item 1: A contribution to the work of the lord

Because the Lord has saved you, forgiven your sins and set you free, you surely want the Gospel of the Lord to reach other people so that they, too, might be saved. You must contribute financially to this. You should, first of all, set that portion apart for the Lord, put it in a special envelope and put it aside before you go on to the rest of the budget. If you do it that way, you will be blessed. The question may arise in your mind on how much you are to give. This is, in a sense, a matter between both of you and the Lord. I think that the minimum should be 10%. I do not see how anyone can decide to do less. If you put God and His Kingdom first, He, too, will put you and your interests first. If you put Him in another position, what do you want Him to do to you? Read the following from the Bible:

"Return to me, and I will return to you, says the Lord of hosts. But you say, 'How shall we return?' Will man rob God? Yet you are robbing me. But you say, 'How are we robbing thee?' In your tithes and offerings. You are cursed with a curse, for you are robbing me; the whole nation of you. Bring the full tithes into the storehouse, that there may be food in my house; and thereby put me to the test, says the Lord of hosts, if I will not open the windows of heaven for you and pour down for you an overflowing blessing. I will rebuke the devourer for you, so that it will not destroy the fruits of your soil; and your vine in the field shall not fail to bear, says the Lord of hosts. Then all nations will call you blessed, for you will be a land of delight, says the Lord of hosts" (Malachi 3:7-12).

"The point is this: he who sows sparingly will also reap sparingly, and he who sows bountifully will also reap bountifully. Each one must do as he has made up his mind, not reluctantly or under compulsion, for God loves a cheerful giver. And God is able to provide you with every blessing in abundance, so that you may always have enough of everything and may provide in abundance for every good work. As it is written, 'He scatters abroad, he gives to the poor; his righteousness endures for ever.' He who supplies seeds to the sower and bread for food will supply and multiply your resources and increase the harvest of your righteousness. You will be enriched in every way for great generosity, which through us will produce thanksgiving to God; for the rendering of this service not only supplies the wants of the saints but also overflows in many thanksgivings to God. Under the test of this service, you will glorify God by your obedience in acknowledging the gospel of Christ, and by the generosity of your contribution for them and for all others; while they long for you and pray for you, because of the surpassing grace of God in you. Thanks be to God for his inexpressible gift" (2 Corinthians 9:6-15).

"Give, and it will be given to you; good measure, pressed down, shaken together, running over, will be put into your lap. For the measure you give will be the measure you get back" (Luke 6:38).

Item 2: Rent

You may be living in your own house and, therefore, paying no rent. This item will, therefore, not be important for you. If you are living with someone who pays rent, make a contribution towards the rent. If you do pay rent, do so promptly. Do not owe the landlord.

Item 3: Food

Enough money should be set aside for the food. Inflation should be taken into account and that sum of money increased as the need arises. All the food money should be given to the wife at the beginning of the financial month and she should control it. She should draw up the menu and see how she can feed the family well at a reasonable cost. She should find out where various items can be bought cheaply, and discuss with others how to feed the family cheaply. She should keep records of her expenditures, as these will be useful when the need arises to increase the food money. It may be necessary to increase the food budget in a month when there are more visitors than usual. Occasionally, there will be shortages. These should be made up for, from the item called 'unforeseen'. If shortages are frequent, then either the money put aside for food is insufficient or the wife is undisciplined or extravagant. Food money must not be used to buy clothes and other things. The wife is not to meet her relatives' needs from there. Food money is for food.

Item 4: Savings

Only the fool eats today and forgets tomorrow. Not to save for tomorrow is a mark of gross indiscipline. Each couple should put aside some of the earnings for future use. I suggest that 10 - 20% of the family income should be saved. If this is not possible, there should still be some savings, even if they are 1%. There will be things like a fridge, a bed, a cooker, a car, etc., to buy which are beyond the monthly provisions of the budget. There may be children to educate, a house to build, etc. Where will the money come from if it has not been saved systematically over a long time? It is not spirituality to use up everything through carelessness and indiscipline and expect the Lord to meet your needs in the future through those who are disciplined. If you do not save, you will possibly borrow. The Bible says, *"Owe no one anything, except to love one another"* (Romans 13:8). No Christian should be in debt. To avoid this, plan systematically for future needs by regular saving.

Item 5: Transportation

This will include taxi fares, the cost of petrol, the repairs of the car and all the items that fall into that group.

Item 6: Water, electricity and gas

Your situation may mean that you do not pay for water, electricity or gas. That item will then disappear from your budget. If you pay for these things, you should use your past experiences to allocate sufficient funds to cover these items.

Item 7: The wife's pocket money

The wife must be given a sum of money which is entirely hers to use as she wants. This is her pocket money. If she chooses to waste it, it is her affair. The husband must not interfere or ask her any questions about it. The sum should take into account all the peculiar needs of a woman. A man should prove his love for his wife by giving her a generous pocket allowance.

Item 8: The husband's pocket money

The same thing that applies to the wife's pocket allowance should apply to the husband's. The husband, as the overall controller of the budget, must be disciplined. He should not use any money outside his pocket money without consulting his wife. This will be unfaithfulness. If he needs extra money because of regular professional needs, these needs should all be taken into account as the budget is being drawn up.

Items 9 and 10: Relatives

The financial needs of the relatives of both the wife and the husband should be studied, and how much the couple wants to be involved discussed and settled prayerfully. It is better to set aside a fixed sum each month for the wife's relatives and for the husband's relatives. The money, when not used, is put aside for the time that need may arise and then it can be used. I recommend that the wife should take charge of the money for her relatives, and the husband the money for his relatives, and that they should each judge who really needs it. Money should then be given as coming from both of them. Neither the family of the husband nor that of the wife must be allowed to exploit the couple through excessive demands. They should be made to understand that anything that is given to them is a privilege and not a right. No couple should borrow money to meet the needs of relatives. This is folly.

Item 11: House-help

The servant working in the house should be regularly and generously paid. There is no substitute for this. Those outside of Christ may exploit them, but you who belong to Jesus must be different.

Item 12: Children's needs

Money should be provided regularly for the clothing and other needs of the children. It is nonsense to expect the wife to use her pocket allowance to buy things for the children.

Item 13: The poor

Some money should be set aside each month to meet the needs of the poor. These should include beggars along the street and any other people who are in need. This is an important item. The Lord Jesus expects it (Matthew 6:2-4).

Item 14: Entertainment

There will be visitors coming to the house regularly. Some money should be set aside for entertaining them, unless the food budget was drawn up with special consideration of this.

Item 15: Unforeseen expenditure

There will be things that come up that were not foreseen. Provision must be made for them, or else the budget will fail. My father taught me to allocate 10% of the budget for unforeseen expenditures and to transfer the money to the budget of the next month if all of it is not used. I have practised this for years and I strongly recommend it to you.

You will find that it pays to work out a budget. The discipline that is needed to do this pays rich dividends and solves many problems. Please, start to plan a budget at once. Put it into action with the next pay. In that way, you will truly enjoy the financial aspect of your married life.

You will notice that the budget does not provide for extra-marital relationships. It does not provide for the rents, clothing, etc., of the loose women outside. This is as it should be. When a man comes to Jesus, he breaks all such relationships, for they are evil. All his money is put into the family. He has nothing to hide. He is free and he is liberated. Jesus is the Liberator. He wants to liberate you today. Will you let Him?

CHAPTER 6

CHILDREN
IN MARRIAGE

Children play an important role in marriage. I have heard people say the following:

1. "This woman is barren and useless. Why did I marry her? She is giving me no children. What shall I do?"

2. "I wish I had done everything to be sure that this woman would bear me children. I was such a fool. I did not investigate. And now I am stuck with her. I will have no alternative but to..."

3. "I never thought that I would ever be married to two women. I always knew that women were a problem. One is enough problems. Now, I have doubled the problems. The problem was the desire for children. I wanted children desperately and I wanted them quickly. We got married. After six months, nothing. After one year zero! After three years, it was just as in the beginning. I then decided that I must hit the iron while it was hot. I married the second woman. It was not because I had stopped loving my first wife. I love her. I will always love her. I do not even love the second woman. But for her children, she would be sent out of my house even this very moment. So I have two of them: one for love and the other one for children. But man! It is perpetual headache. I used to be a special man to my first wife. There was something special in her heart for me. It seems that when the second woman came in, something in her heart and in her relationship with me died. I wish it were back."

4. "Please Doctor, can you help me? I married the girl I loved and who loved me. We did not have children quickly. My family began to mock me, saying that I had married

a decoration for my house. I was unhappy. At moments their comments made me despise my wife, even though I loved her. In order not to disappoint my family members, I got married to another girl of our tribe. Their plan was that I would eventually send away the first wife, since polygamy is for primitive people. Two months after I got married to the second woman, both became pregnant. They both have children now. I look at my first wife and her children and I feel satisfied. I look at the second woman and her children and wish that neither she nor her children were there. What shall I do?

5.   "My first wife gave me no children. My second wife also gave me no children. I am very angry with them. I have invested my money on them, yet what is my gain? I think of a third wife, but I am worried. There are three problems. The first one is that the bride price is very heavy in my tribe. I may be permanently ruined by the cost of a third wife. Secondly, I may make a mistake in choosing and again marry the woman who will give me no children. Thirdly, the first two wives are a bore to my life. How will I stand the addition of a third one to them?"

6.   "My husband blamed me night and day because we had no children after nine years of marriage. He went out with other women because he said that I was good for nothing. I felt very frustrated and decided that I would also go out. I committed adultery twice and now I find that I am pregnant. What am I to do? He does not yet know that I am pregnant. Shall I tell him all the truth? I feel totally miserable that what I have longed for for nine years should happen and instead bring shame. What help is there for me?"

7.   "My husband is always blaming me for giving birth to girls. He says that he may bring in a second woman who will give him boys."

8.   "I never intended to have many children. We had planned to have only four. But it turned out that the first four were girls. Since we wanted boys we went on, and now we have twelve daughters and I feel a deep sense of failure."

9.   "I intended that we should have only three children because of my poor financial situation. My wife was not quite in agreement with me. She wanted twelve children. I talked her into agreeing with me. She finally nodded and I rejoiced because I thought that she had at last agreed with me. She went to see a doctor for family planning. He put her on the pill. However, we now have six children at a regular interval of two years. I believe that my wife is at the root of it and that I have been tricked."

10.   "My parents sent me away at the age of three to live with my grandmother. I did not like her. She was wrinkled and very old and I used to get frightened because she looked very much like a witch. There was no communication between us. I worked very hard to satisfy her, but I withdrew completely into myself. I lived with her until I was twelve and then I came back to my parents. I find that I am so different from the other children of my parents. I am withdrawn while they are outgoing. I hesitate before I do anything. They are fast going. To make things worse, people say that my manners and attitudes are like those of a grandmother. Some call me the 'baby granny.' I am very miserable."

11. "My parents left me with my uncle and his wife when I was six months old and went to Britain to study. When they came back, I could not recognise them as my parents. They took me to their home. I do not know how to put it, but something was destroyed in me then. I am twenty-one years old now and people say that I am beautiful, but I hate people. I hate my parents. I hate life. I have tried to kill myself twice, but it did not work. I would do it all over if I could. I do not want to live. Nobody really loves me. I doubt everybody. I doubt myself. Why should I live?"

12. "My father is orderly and disciplined. My mother is disorderly and undisciplined. There is always a cold war going on between them about how the bed is made, the shoes placed, the clothes hung, the chairs arranged, the kitchen kept, the food served, the children dressed, the books arranged, etc. They are good people, but as I look at them I can see that their differences have ruined their lives. I am torn in between the two. I want to be as orderly and disciplined as my father; for I know this is right, but I am always with my mother and there is no way in which she can become disciplined and orderly. Slowly, I am becoming disorderly and undisciplined, and this is slowly separating me from my father whom I love and who loves me."

13. "My parents let me do anything I wanted. They never stopped me. They said that I should be totally free in order to be freely developed and not have inhibitions. I was very happy that way. I did everything I wanted. I destroyed things and wasted some and they took it well. My problem is that in school things must be done in an orderly way

and on time. I cannot go out to play any time I want. I must study subjects that I do not want. I must not talk whenever I want. I hate school. I hate the teachers. They are standing in the way of my freedom."

14.   "When I do something bad and my mother wants to beat me, my father steps in, bullies her and sets me free. I am very glad about this. My father is a wonderful man, but I do not like my mother. Sometimes I wonder if she is my mother."

15.   "My father forced me to do things correctly. I had to study even when I did not want to study. He only gave me money when there was a real need and, even then, I had to give a detailed account of how the money was spent. This meant that I could not do the things that my friends were doing then. I did not like my father then. I thought he did not love me. However, now I can see all the difference. My life is much better than that of the other boys. I have got a better job, a happier life, etc., than most people. My father was wonderful. He was right. I will try to treat my children the way he treated me."

Children in marriage

Children are a gift from God to those who are married. Because they are gifts, He is not under obligation to give children to all couples. To think of children as a right is to be seriously mistaken. Children can be a serious liability to a couple and cause them much misery. He, therefore, blesses that couple by giving them no children. I have known couples whose lives have been ruined by their children. Some children have caused perpetual heartache to their parents. Think of the boy who grows up and kills his father; think of the daughter who ends up as a prostitute; think of the child who ends up totally crippled so that he has to be fed, dressed, taken to the toilet, etc., and throughout his life he cannot do anything for himself. The parents of such children would have had a more fulfilled life without those children. Children are not always a blessing. There is the other matter, the service of the Lord. There are situations in life in which the call of God to service may be better answered and fulfilled by a couple that has no children. Such can then wholeheartedly commit themselves to the work of the Lord without distractions.

No one should be married to a partner who hasn't all that he needs to satisfy him/her. No one is to be married so that his wife and his children may satisfy him. If your partner-to-be has not got all that it takes to satisfy you, just leave him/her alone. Do not accept him or her on condition that his or her deficiencies will be made up for by the presence of children. Only marry someone with whom you will find total fulfilment with or without children.

For those couples who have no children, I recommend the following:

1 Find out if your childlessness is owing to some sin you have committed in the past, be it before or after marriage. For example, if you committed the sin of fornication, adultery, abortion, etc.; if you suffered from venereal disease, you might have personally contributed to your present situation.

The first thing you should do is not to ask God to give you children, but to recognise the fact that you sinned against God and are separated from Him. You are under His judgment. Repent of the sins you committed. Confess each of them to God; ask Him to forgive you. He is willing to do so because Jesus died on the cross in your place. Turn to Jesus. He is not far from you. Ask Him to come into your life as your Lord and Saviour. If you do this, the Lord will come into your life immediately and make you His child. You can then be sure that your sins are forgiven and that God is now prepared to deal with their consequences. If both of you have repented, and I urge both of you to repent, you should both kneel down before the Lord and pray to Him in the following way:

"Lord God, our sins led us into this situation of childlessness. You have forgiven our sins and washed them away in the blood of Jesus. Now, Lord, please take away this childlessness which is a consequence of those sins and heal our reproductive systems. Lord, give us children from now on according to Your will." The Lord will hear your prayer and give you children.

If you have been trying to get children through the help of sorcerers and witch-doctors, abandon these people and all that they have given you, and look to the Lord. God is more than all these people and He will do what they cannot do. If you have believed but your partner has not yet believed, go ahead and pray the above prayer, and God will hear you while you continue to look to Him for the conversion of your partner.

2 If you did not commit any of the sins mentioned above, you
   may have committed other ones, including perhaps, stealing,
   anger, wickedness, bitterness, pride, lying, pretending, etc.
   These sins place you out of contact with God, so that He
   cannot hear you. The Lord told people in Bible times and still
   tells you today:

*"Behold, the Lord's hand is not shortened, that it cannot save, or his
ear dull, that it cannot hear; but your iniquities (sins) have made a
separation between you and your God, and your sins have hid his
face from you so that he does not hear. For your hands are defiled
with blood and your fingers with iniquity; your lips have spoken lies,
your tongue mutters wickedness"* (Isaiah 59:1-3).

So repent of all your sins. Turn to the Lord. Receive Jesus
Christ as your Lord and Saviour. Then pray to Him and wait
on Him. He will richly bless you.

3 If you have already received the Lord Jesus, be fully occupied
   with serving Him. Try to tell everyone about Him. Contribute financially to the work of the Gospel. Be occupied with
   God's business and He will be occupied with yours.

Polygamy and childlessness

Polygamy is not the perfect will of God. He allowed people to practise it in the Old Testament time in His permissive will, but His standard is: one man, one wife. He gave Adam one wife as His perfect example. He says that the two shall become one flesh and not that the three or four shall become one flesh. It is not God's will that a person should marry a second wife because the first one does not yet have children. In the Bible, there are women who did not have children early in their marriage to whom, afterwards, God gave children. Sarah, Rebecca, Rachel, Hannah, Elizabeth are only some of the examples. Some of them had children after very many years of marriage. Sarah was childless for most of her married life. Rebecca had her first child after twenty years of married life. When we are dealing with a miracle-working God, no woman is too old for the miracle of God to operate and give her children.

The other side of the matter is that there are many couples whose childlessness is due to a problem with the man. There are many sterile men whose sterility may be from birth or from venereal diseases. Should a wife take a second husband because the first one could not give her children? When a couple is childless, they should both seek medical advice to determine where the problem is. Then, it is useless to blame the party who has a problem. The best way is to seek a solution from medical science. There are, however, many cases where medical science has not been able to solve the problem. Are these cases hopeless? No, they are not hopeless. I know of many couples that could not have children and medical science had given them up. They turned to the Lord Jesus and we prayed with them and Jesus Christ, the Lord of science, did what science could not do. He gave them children. He is willing to do that for you. If you have a problem in that area, please write to me.

Unfairness to women

In our society the women are treated very unfairly. When a couple is childless the woman is immediately held to be the culprit. When the children are all girls, she is held to be the cause, even though the sex-determining factor is provided by the man and not by the woman. When the children are all boys, she is again blamed. A girl must be a virgin at marriage but the man is not expected to be so; a woman must be faithful in marriage but the man can have extra-marital experiences. The wife must remain beautiful and slim while the man can become pregnant with alcohol. These double standards are not accepted by the Lord who sees all, records all and will bring both man and woman to equal judgment.

Receiving children

Children are to be received as gifts from the Lord. They are to be received with great fear and trembling. They are amongst God's greatest gifts to man, but they are gifts for which the greatest account to God will have to be made.

Each child is a sacred trust, to be loved, brought up in the fear of the Lord and for the glory of the Lord. That is why both parents ought to turn radically from all sin and make a radical commitment of their lives to the Lord in order to be able to learn from Him how to bring up the children that He has given to them and in the way that He wants. In the following paragraphs I am going to assume that you have received the Lord Jesus as your Lord and Saviour and that you are committed to obeying Him in every area of your life. We then want to look at the bringing up of children.

1 The best way to bring up children is to provide a love-filled home for them. The best thing that a man can do for his children is to love their mother deeply and respect her. The best thing that a woman can do for her children is to love the children as nobody else can. Children from broken homes tend to be broken. Children from homes where cold wars, open wars, quarrels, harsh words and the like are common are also broken to some extent. Because the Lord Jesus is able to fill a man's heart with love and respect for his wife and do the same for the wife, He is the obvious answer to this.

2 Children learn from what they see. They will grow up to be like you. Even if they do not see what you are in private or in hiding, they will be like you. This is a law. Many of the faults of children can be traced back to their parents and grandparents and even great-grandparents.

If you are a thief, your children will most likely become thieves.

If you are an adulterer or adulteress, your children will become like you.

If you are holy, your children will most likely follow you in the path of holiness.

If you are lazy, they will become lazy.

If you are generous, they will become generous.

If you are a liar, they will become liars.

If you are honest, they will tend to become honest. If you insult your wife, they will insult theirs.

If you love and respect your wife, they will tend to do the same, etc.

The truth is that children hold their parents in such high esteem that they will consciously or unconsciously do what they see their parents do. In addition, there is what I may call "habit genes." What parents are is somehow passed to the children, even when the children do not see their parents doing those things. Your secret life will be handed over. Have you thought about it? Take time and ponder over this matter. Think of all the things you have done. Think of your sons and daughters doing the same things. Does the thought bring peace to your heart? Do not shake it off and just say that it is their affair. It is your affair because you are by your conduct making history. You are making generations upon generations to come. It is a common observation that children from broken marriages normally have broken marriages. Illegitimate children normally end up producing illegitimate children. The popular pop star singer sang, "What papa is doing is what mama will do." I add to this, "What papa and mama are is what the children will be." You are, second by second, making history. What will that history be in the third,

fourth and fifth generations? Think about it. Please, think. If you
give your life to Jesus and walk in His ways, you will by your life
set an example for your children, which will be a blessing in all
of the future.

3 Lead your children to the Lord Jesus. Teach them the
Word of God. Teach them to pray. Teach them to give to the
work of the Lord. As soon as they begin to understand, start pre-
senting the claims of Jesus to them. Be sensitive to the Holy Spirit. Ask them if they want to repent and be saved. Children understand spiritual things a lot more clearly than adults. When our
daughter was almost four years old, a friend of hers who was
eight years old and had believed, died. Our daughter asked
where her friend had gone to. She was told that she had gone to
be with Jesus in heaven. She said that she, too, wanted to be sure
that when she died she would go to heaven to be with Jesus. She
was led to the Lord and she has been God's child since then. She
is growing in grace. She is not perfect, but the work of grace is
progressing in her life. The same thing has happened to four of
our five children, and it has happened before any of them was
eight years old. Our first daughter was baptised before she was
eight. She received the gift of speaking in tongues and has
continued to pray and praise in a heavenly language since then
until today, three years since that first experience. Recently,
when I shut myself up to pray with my two older boys, aged 9
and 7, and our daughter, I was amazed by the change that had
taken place in them. The first boy had always wanted to be a pre-
sident and the second wanted to be a policeman. This time both
boys wanted to be pastors. I asked them why they wanted to be
pastors and they said that it is because they want to preach the
Gospel. I asked them what they would do if people did not be-

lieve and the second immediately said that he would continue to preach. Our daughter of five (who had believed just before she was four) said with tears in her eyes that she wanted to serve the Lord. We had a wonderful prayer time. Each prayed and then I prayed. The presence of the Holy Spirit was there and He was upon us. In a new way, Prisca and I have a solemn responsibility to bring up these children so that they will grow up to serve the Lord in a most total way.

I think back to my own early hunger after God. In 1952 when I was seven years old, I remember my father preaching a message on the new birth. He said that as the wind blew and no one knew from where it came and to where it went, so was a person born of the Holy Spirit. I longed to be born again. That afternoon I went to the field and walked round and round, trying to start and go in a direction which no one could tell. I wanted to enter into the experience but I could not ask my father. I was not satisfied. I asked another pastor's son, Peter Ekwoge, who was older than I how I could be sure that I would go to heaven when I died. He told me that when I died God would immediately show me two lists. On one would be written all the sins I had committed and on the other would be written all the good things that I had done. The list that was longer would decide where I would go. If my sins were more than my good deeds, I would go to hell, but if my good deeds were more, I would go to heaven. So for the next years I tried to do as much good as possible and as little evil as possible and, thereby, hoped that I would make it to heaven. This continued until 1955 when I was ten years old. My father, who used to receive and distribute tracts that were produced in America, one day gave me a tract entitled, "Some One Died for You." This tract explained that Jesus had died for me and that I should receive Him and be saved. I followed the three steps outlined in that tract and invited Jesus into my life. Joy filled my heart and I immediately ran to the village one mile away to tell my friend (Reuben Unota) that Jesus had died for him. A hunger to read God's Word was born in my heart and by the time I went to the Secondary School in January, 1960, I had read the entire Bible twice over. There were times when I read the Word up to 2am. I used to take my father's old Bible and underline the verses that he had underlined in his Bible in mine. In the Secondary School, I prayed and carried out many religious and Christian activities. I was living for the Lord in part, but I lived mainly for myself. I wanted to be famous. I wanted to earn a doctorate's degree. My heart was divided. I had no assurance of salvation. I lied and would have liked to commit fornication. The only thing that kept me back was the fear that such a thing would bring terrible shame to my beloved Daddy whom I loved and idolised. So, although there was not much outward sin, my heart was rotten. When I got to the University, I saw the rottenness of my heart, turned radically to Jesus, gave Him the master-key of my life and dedicated myself to love and serve Him, and I have never withdrawn from that surrender. Immediately after that commitment, I knew for the first time that I was indeed a child of God, that my sins were washed away permanently and that my name was written in the book of life once and for all.

As I look back, I know that if I had been helped on that day in 1952 when I first heard that sermon on the new birth, I would have been born again then and, if I had been led into an assurance of salvation, I would have loved the Lord and lived for Him from the age of seven. Oh! How much time would have been gained from the service of Satan and self for the service of the Lord Jesus and the Gospel!

So, at the earliest age, lead your child to Jesus. If you are sensitive to the Lord and His Spirit, you will be able to tell when the Holy Spirit has done the basic work of conviction of sin and revealing of the Lord Jesus, and you will know how and when to act. You should take their commitment seriously, teach them about baptism into water and they will ask to be baptised. Baptise them immediately and lay hands on them and the Holy Spirit will come upon them, often faster than upon adults. Do not be guided by the traditions of men and bar your children from coming to Christ or from being baptised after they have believed. Be bold and lay hands on them and ask Jesus the Baptiser to baptise them into the Holy Spirit. After that, let them break bread with other believers. On the other hand, if you baptise them as babies or before they have believed, you are deceiving them, and you will answer for it. The Bible says, *"Repent and be baptized every one of you (children included) in the name of Jesus Christ for the forgiveness of your sins; and you shall receive the gift of the Holy Spirit. For the promise is to you and to your children and to all that are far off, every one whom the Lord our God calls to him"* (Acts 2: 38-39).

4 Pray with your children. Pray with them as a group. Pray with each one alone. Both of you should pray for them and each one of you should pray for them. This is the primary duty of parents to their children. In prayer, pray all God's will for them to come to pass.

5 Teach them to work hard. Let them learn to wash plates, clean the floor, wash clothes, clean the yard, make their beds, etc., even if there are people who could do these things. Plan things well and let each child know what his responsibilities are. This should be done from the age of three. If they are not trained to work hard from childhood, it will be much more difficult to do so later on. Bear in mind that work does not destroy. Those who work in childhood are the better for it. Looking back at my own life, I went to work on the farm after school every day from the age of seven, except when it was raining. All Saturdays and all holidays were spent on the farm. At home I boiled water for my father to bathe before 5 a.m. from the age of nine. I pounded fufu, grated cassava for the making of garri, sold "akra" from the age of seven, etc., and I think I am the better for all these things. My father worked hard and forced us to work hard. My only fear is that I am not having my children to work that hard. "Lord, help me not to fail You and fail my children in so serious a matter."

6 Discipline your children. Rebuke them when they need rebuke. Punish them when they need it. You can punish them by withdrawing some privilege for some time, provided you let them know that it is punishment. Make sure that you do restore the privilege when the punishment is over. One such punishment could be to let the guilty child stay at home while you take the others out for a ride or a walk. It may be necessary to lock the one who is being punished in a room alone for some minutes, hours, and even a day depending on the gravity of the wrong. Another thing is to beat them with a cane. My father had a good cane in the house always and he used it for this purpose. They could also be punished by giving them more practical work or making them do some academic work which they must finish when the others are having recreation. Another thing is that they could be prevented from having a meal or two, even three. For proper discipline, they should be placed in circumstances where they cannot have food by some fraudulent means. Each family should decide which method of punishment is to be used and which combination is effective.

Both parents must agree on the discipline. No parent should release a child from discipline that has been imposed by the other one. No parent should be made to appear as the loving one by not disciplining the children, and no parent should be made to appear as the wicked one by pushing all the disciplining to him. The mother who says, "Wait, your father will come and you will have it," is failing in her responsibility. It is better for discipline to follow immediately after the crime. However, major acts of discipline should be the husband's responsibility.

Discipline should be corrective. The child should not be punished because the parent is angry. The child should be made to see the wrong that he has done. Then the punishment should be announced. Then the parent should pray that the punishment should accomplish the purpose for which it is intended. After that the punishment should be administered. All this should be done in a calm spirit. No parent should allow himself to be controlled by anger.

After the punishment has been administered, the child should be comforted and loved and restored and the whole incident forgotten completely.

There are some who do not see the necessity to discipline. This is folly. The Bible says: *"Do not withhold discipline from a child; if you beat him with a rod, he will not die. If you beat him with the rod you will save his life from Sheol"* (Proverbs 23:13-14). *"Train up a child in the way he should go, and when he is old he will not depart from it"* (Proverbs 22: 6).

"Discipline your son while there is hope, do not set your heart on his destruction" (Proverbs 19:18). *"He who spares the rod hates his son, but he who loves him is diligent to discipline him"* (Proverbs 13:24).

"Folly is bound up in the heart of a child, but the rod of discipline drives it far from him" (Proverbs 22:15).

7 Encourage your child. The Bible says, *"Fathers, do not provoke your children, lest they become discouraged"* (Colossians 3:21). Parents should encourage their children. When the child does something that is good, he should be approved. The good traits in a child should be discovered and the child helped to develop them.

8 Allow the children to grow up into individuals of their own. Children should not be forced to be something else from what they were meant to be. Sometimes parents want to force their children to become what they themselves failed to become. "Become a great doctor, lawyer, businessman, etc.," are often thoughts that are driven into children by the parents, and children are forced to try to be something that will satisfy the ego of the parents. Have you thought about the fact that your child may fulfil his destiny by being a driver, a carpenter, etc., without becoming the "great man" that you want? A wise parent will encourage the child to develop the abilities that he has. He will never discourage the child from developing the abilities that he has. He will never discourage the child by comparing him unfavourably with another child. I have heard parents say to the children, "You are a fool. Your classmates are already in secondary school and you are here in class five, wasting my money for nothing!" These are tragic words. May they never come out of your lips.

Family size

The husband and wife should prayerfully determine before God how many children He wants them to have. After that number is reached, the proper medical techniques should be used to avoid the arrival of more children. God wants the earth to be replenished, but not overpopulated! To bring more children into the world than you can adequately provide for spiritually, emotionally and materially is folly and not spirituality. The Bible says that the one who does not provide for his household has denied the faith and is worse than an infidel (I Timothy 5:8). To have children for whom you cannot adequately provide is like denying the faith and becoming worse than an infidel. Providing for the family is not just material. It is also spiritual and emotional.

Bring up your own children

Each husband and wife have the responsibility before God to bring up their own children so that they grow up to be like them. To send one's children to be brought up by others is folly. They may be sent to live with rich relatives or friends, but the facilities will never make up for what the children are missing from their parents. The child should grow up to resemble his parents and not the aunt, uncle or friend. If a child's parents are dead, then the child can be received into another home, but this must be on the personal initiative of the husband and wife in the new home who would commit themselves to love the child and give him all that they can.

Obeying parents

The Bible commands children to obey their parents. It says, *"Children, obey your parents in the Lord, for this is right. 'Honour your father and mother.'* (this is the first commandment with a promise), *'that it may be well with you and that you may live long on the earth'"* (Ephesians 6:1-3). God has promised to bless children who obey their parents. All children should obey their parents and so be blessed by God. This obedience is a proof of the child's submission to divinely instituted authority. The child is also to honour - give respect, take care of and contribute all that can be contributed, to make the life of the parents happy and fulfilled. I have often thought that the best way to honour one's parents is to abstain from sin. Children who commit fornication, adultery, theft, and all the things that God hates bring dishonour to their parents. Children should encourage their parents and love them. They should labour to spend some time with them and, when they are old, they should do all that they can to take care of them.

The obedience to parents is to be in the Lord. That is to say that it is to be obedience that God approves of, obedience that brings glory to the Lord. This means that parents should be seen as God's delegated authority. All authority is dependent on obedience. So, we have,

God's authority and commandment

↓

God's authority handed to parents who obey him

↓

God's authority exercised by these parents over children

↓

Children yield to this authority and, thereby,
satisfy parents and God.

So the authority of God is handed over by Him to parents to be exercised over the children on His behalf. Authority is obtained and maintained by obedience. Parents who yield to God in everything and obey Him in everything wield great authority and power over their children. Children must obey such parents. If not, they will have problems, not only with their parents, but with God. Children who disobey such parents are disobeying God, and God will not let them go unpunished. They will be punished sooner or later on.

However, if parents disobey God, if they put away God's truth and live their lives in rebellion to God, they lose their God-given authority over the children and should not be obeyed.

Children must not obey parents who are themselves disobeying God. Children must not obey parents in doing anything that God forbids. Before a child obeys the parents, he must ask himself if that obedience will also be an obedience to God. If it is so, the child must obey at once. If the command of the parents is contrary to that of God, the child must show his love and loyalty to parents and God by obeying the higher authority (God) and, thereby, putting aside the commands of the delegated authority (the parents). God will stand by such a child and bless him for his obedience to Him (God) and his disobedience to them (the parents). So when there is conflict between the demands of God and the demands of parents, it is also a matter of choice between the blessing of God and the blessing of parents; between the curse of God and the curse of parents.

If parents curse children who obey God rather than them, the curse is rendered of no effect by God. If God curses a child who obeys his parents rather than Him, who can nullify the curse?

Normally, there should be no conflicts between the demands of God and the demands of parents. However, they sometimes arise. In such cases the Son of God says, *"Do not think that I have come to bring peace on earth; I have not come to bring peace, but a sword. For I have come to set a man against his father, and a daughter against her mother, and a daughter-in-law against her mother-in-law; and a man's foes will be those of his own household. He who loves father or mother more than me is not worthy of me; and he who loves son or daughter more than me is not worthy of me; and he who does not take his cross and follow me is not worthy of me. He who finds his life will lose it, and he who loses his life for my sake will find it"* (Matthew 10:34-39).

The conflict which Jesus talks about here is actually caused by those who disobey God. If father, mother and children all asked what God wanted in a particular situation; if they sought God's will and did it, then there would be peace and harmony.

If you are the parent or child who is disobeying God's will and God's Word, then you are the author of division.

I remember a man who came to see me one day. His son was finishing a Master of Philosophy thesis in Organic Chemistry under my supervision and had fallen in love with an undergraduate student in the liberal arts discipline. This father, although he has a diploma from a University abroad, told me, "I do not want my son to marry that undergraduate. I have decided that he must marry Miss... who is from my village and is at the Secondary School at...." I looked at him and wondered for whom the wife was meant to be - for the father or for the son? I asked him if his son had a part in the choice and he told me, "I want him to marry a girl who will give me a place of honour in my village." It is needless to say that such self-centred parents are not acting well as God's delegated authority, and they can be disobeyed without breaking God's law.

Amen.

CHAPTER 7

SERVANTS
IN A MARRIAGE HOME

There is an increasing number of homes where someone or some people are employed to work as servants. They may be employed by the State or employed by the husband and wife. These people fall in the general class that I call servants. In another sense, a servant is anyone who serves another. I am a servant of the Lord Jesus. I am also a servant of the University of Yaounde. Many of the things that will be said about house servants apply to all servants in general, but we will limit ourselves to servants in a home and their impact on the marriage.

There is a very sad situation today in many homes.

The husband works from 7.30 to 12.00 and then from 2.30 to 5.30. The wife also works for the same number of hours. This means that the children are really being brought up by the servants. Whether or not the financial benefits from the wife's salary compensate for the harm that may possibly be done to the children needs to be carefully looked into. I can only say that it is very sad that a child should be at its most tender and most formative years in the hands of a hired servant. She is often there for a few months or a year and then another one has to come in, each one different from the previous one, and the children have to bear the impact of these changes. The result can only be disastrous. I am not going to ask the modern housewife to put her children before her career or to sacrifice the career for the children. I am not going to ask a luxury-loving couple in a disorientated world to cut down their luxury and let the wife stay at home and take care of the children, instead of the servants. I will not suggest these two things, although they are necessary. I will not be heard. The facts of inflation and the need for this and that are pressing and too many; such that what must be sacrificed is the children. The generation that is brought up by house-girls will soon show itself, and we shall reap what we are sowing! Because house-servants are here to stay, I must write this chapter in the light of that reality.

There are a number of things to do in the recruitment of house-helps and their work in the home, and I want to address myself, first of all, to the husbands and wives.

1 - Recruitment

Since the future of your children and, to a certain extent, your happiness as a couple, will be influenced very greatly by the character and habits of the person you employ to work in your house, be careful as to whom you select. Look at the person's past record. The person who has moved from one home to another and from one town to another is most likely a problem character. Beware! She is likely to have an advanced diploma in comparison and, instead of working for you, will be comparing you with other people. So, look at their credentials. Look into her habits. It is best to establish a contract that gives a three-month trial period for either parties. She will try you to see if she can work with you and you will try her to see if she can work with you. This trial period will be used to see if she is clean or dirty, hard-working or lazy, kind to children or unkind to them, tender or harsh, polite or rude, respectful or disrespectful, etc. You certainly know what you want and you should be careful. Since her main duty will be to help the mistress of the house to do her work and not the mistress helping her to do her work, the nature of the relationship that is building up between her and the mistress should be studied. If the house-help is a person with her own ideas, who wants to do what she wants, who will readily lay aside definite instructions and do things her own way, then to employ her permanently would be to court disaster. Her attitude to things should also be studied. If she is extravagant with food, oil, water, electricity, and if she is careless with plates, cups, carpets, etc., then those who employ her should fully be aware of what they are getting in for. The three months probation will enable many of these areas to be discerned. Things should then be discussed afresh. She should be asked how she feels: if she is happy and wants to stay or if she would prefer to go away. If she opts to stay, she should be shown her faults and how to amend them. The wife should now commit herself to teach the servant what to do. The attitude of many wives, which is to give commands to servants to do things that they have not been taught how they are to be done, is not to be recommended. Remember that the servant is there to help the wife to keep her (the wife's) house and not the wife to help the servant. So the wife must do things herself. She must also teach the servant. If she is to cook, the wife should first cook the type of dish in question while showing the servant what to do. It is not wise to expect that she will master it after watching the mistress do it once. I suggest that there should be a second session in which it is done with the servant acting as an assistant. The third time, it should be done by the servant with the mistress looking on to offer corrections and helpful criticisms. When the servant has mastered it well enough, she can now be expected to do it when asked to. This principle of teaching the servant should apply to everything that she will be expected to do, be it going to the market, cleaning the floor, washing clothes, taking care of children, etc. No servant should be blamed or held responsible for doing things wrongly if she has not been clearly taught how to do them well.

If after the probation period either party decides that the job should not be confirmed, the servant should be paid two months salary in addition to the salary for the three months during which she has worked. This will enable her to live honourably while looking for the next job. Just to send her away without a thought about her future is wickedness.

2 - Salary

Those who want good servants must be prepared to pay well for them. Servants with the right character and habits are in high demand, and if you are anxious to save your money, you will have one of those cheap ones with poor records and poor performances. I suggest that the husband and wife should look into this very carefully. They should not give the servant the lowest possible salary. They should think of the salary that they would like to earn if they were servants. They should also consider the fact that some day they may be in need or their children may be in need and may have to serve as servants. How would they want them to be treated? So, a reasonable salary should be paid and there should be regular increments. An occasional monetary gift would not be a bad idea, but the servant should be made to depend on her salary and no more. The salary should be paid on a fixed day each month, and it should be paid without the servant having to ask for it. It is normal that it is paid on the family budget day. The servant should be helped on how to spend her money. She should be taught to save for the future, preferably in a bank. I think it helpful for the mistress to keep the bank book in order to avoid temperamental expenditures. Other details as to leave, salary, transportation home, etc., should be sorted out at the time of employment so that both parties know where they stand.

3 - Work load

The work load of a servant should be carefully looked into. There are lazy servants who will complain of any amount of work. They are to be sent out of work. There are, on the other hand, servants who are crushed by work.

To exploit the servant by overworking her is wrong. One servant should not be made to do the work of three servants and yet earn the salary of one servant. This is often the case with lazy wives who are too heavy to stand up and do work, but expect the servant to do everything. If the wife, the husband and the children each participate in the work of the house, then there will be a good time for all. As the number of children increases and they are still too young to render help with housework, the recruitment of another house-help should be considered and acted upon.

4 - The future of the servant

Nobody wants to remain a servant all his life. I suggest that the husband and wife should think of the best way possible for improving the life of their servant. They should do this by sending her to evening school or helping her to learn some trade at hours that are free and previously agreed upon. The husband and wife should take this as a challenge to leave a positive impact on the servant that will bear marks in all of her future life. It is very bad for the husband and wife to think only of themselves and their children. The servant is also a person and the child of someone. So, she must be treated with love and kindness. She must be treated the way you would want your own child treated.

5 - Relationship with the servant

My recommendation is that the wife should have all the direct dealings with the servant and her authority over the servant clearly established. After all, she has to encounter the servant and work with her very directly, whereas the husband's contact with the servant is more remote. The wife should be the one to hand the servant's salary to her. I permit no man to have any close contact with a servant. If the servant is young, pretty and unmarried, there may be an added problem for undisciplined husbands. We all know too well of cases where the servant replaced the wife or became the second wife. If the wife discovers that something fishy is beginning to develop between her husband and her house-servant, she should dismiss her at once and pay her three months salary.

The husband, wife and children should treat the servant with respect. They should neither be harsh nor hard on her. They should do all to make her life happy. The children should be taught to treat her with respect. She should be given freedom to know God and serve Him. She should have some time each week as free time during which she can go wherever she wants and do anything that she wants. There are times when she will be in low moods. Such times should be recognised and she should be treated kindly.

Masters are servants who will give account some day

All earthly masters are servants of God and they have been given the responsibility to be masters by the Lord. He will sooner or later call them back to Himself to give account of their work as masters. So, husband and wife, you will appear before God one day to give account of many things in your life, including the way you have treated your servants. The Bible says, *"Masters, treat your slaves* (servants) *justly and fairly, knowing that you also have a master in heaven"* (Colossians 4: 1). *"It is appointed for men to die once, and after that comes judgment"* (Hebrews 9:27). *"Then I saw a great white throne and him who sat upon it; from his presence earth and sky fled away, and no place was found for them. And I saw the dead great and small, standing before the throne, and books were opened. Also, another book was opened, which is the book of life. And the dead were judged by what was written in the books, by what they had done. And the sea gave up the dead in it, Death and Hades gave up the dead in them, and all were judged by what they had done.*

Then Death and Hades were thrown into the lake of fire. This is the second death, the lake of fire; and if anyone's name was not found written in the book of life, he was thrown into the lake of fire" (Revelation 20:11-15).

You will be judged for the way you treat your servant. You will also be judged for all your other sins. If you are serving the devil now, you will be sent to hell to continue to serve him there. If you are serving him now, then it means that he is your master. You can change masters. You can become a child of God and a servant of the Lord Jesus. You can have all the sins of your past, present and future life covered. Why not acknowledge to God now that you are a sinner? Why not confess your sins to God now? Jesus died on the cross in order to pay for your pardon. On the basis of His death on the cross for you, your sins can all be forgiven now. Confess them to God now. Forsake them now and always. Ask Jesus to come into your life now and be your Saviour and Lord. Immediately He comes in, He will also give you the power and ability to relate to your servant as God wants you to. It will lead to a better relationship from which your entire family will benefit.

To the servant

You have accepted a job in that family on very clear terms. You were not forced into it. You should determine to do an excellent job. There is no choice about it. Unless you work hard in an obedient spirit, you will be thrown out, therefore,

1 Put away laziness. Work hard. You will be all the better for it.

2 Treat your master and mistress with respect. You will gain if you do so. If you are disrespectful, you will not gain anything positive from it. Besides, you may earn a salary of joblessness. Never treat your mistress as your equal. She may be younger than you, but she is the mistress. She may be less experienced than you are, but please obey her. She is the mistress and you are the servant. You may make suggestions, but you should not be disappointed when they are rejected. Do not allow a quarrel to come up between the mistress and you. If you allow such a situation to develop, you will leave the house (and not she), irrespective of who is right. Treat the property carefully. Do not be wasteful. Refrain from extravagant use of things. Do not manifest your anger towards the way they are treating you by wasting and destroying their things. This would be meanness and wickedness. They will punish you for it or get you to pay for your folly.

3 Do not discuss what you see happening in the house with others. If they quarrel, do not tell anyone about it. Do not express your dissatisfaction to other people. If you are dissatisfied, talk to the mistress. If things do not change, talk to the husband. If things cannot improve, you should resign.

4 Know your character faults and do something about them; if not, they will destroy you and your job. Put on humility, joy, self-control, etc., and then you will have no problems. If you have problems with this couple, you may have problems with the next and the next.

5 If you do not want the job any more, please resign and go away without trying to cause problems because you want another one.

6 God has a word for you. He says, *"Slaves (Servants), be obedient to those who are your earthly masters, with fear and trembling, in singleness of heart, as to Christ; not in the way of eye-service, as men-pleasers, but as servants of Christ, doing the will of God from the heart, rendering service with a good will as to the Lord and not to men, knowing that whatever good any one does, he will receive the same again from the Lord, whether he is a slave (servant) or free"* (Ephesians 6:5-8). God says that you should serve your earthly masters as follows:

a.   with obedience.

b.   with fear; with deep respect.

c.   with trembling.

d.   in singleness of heart; totally, completely, not half-heartedly.

e.   in the same way as you would serve Christ.

f.   without thought as to whether they are present and can see you or not. God is looking at you.

g.   let your service reflect what is in your heart, with all goodwill.

h.   God will pay you for your service. You will receive some salary and reward from man, but you should know that the service you are really rendering is not just to man but to Christ, and that He will reward you on the day of judgment.

7 To do the will of God from the heart, to serve man as you would Christ, to be obedient and humble, you need Jesus to wash away your sins, take away your proud nature and give you His humility. When He comes into your heart, He will begin to transform you into the type of person that He wants you

to be and, as you satisfy Him, you will also be satisfying the demands of your earthly masters, which are necessarily lower than those of Christ.

8 You can receive the Lord Jesus Christ into your heart now by faith, believing that He will do all that He promised in the Bible. He says in the Bible, *"Behold, I stand at the door and knock; if anyone hears my voice and opens the door, I will come in to him and eat with him, and he with me"* (Revelation 3:20). So confess all the sins you have committed to God and ask Him to forgive you. Invite Jesus to come into your life. He says, *"Him who comes to me I will not cast out"* (John 6:37).

If you receive Jesus, you will have eternal life. He will give you His heart and nature that will make it easy for you to be humble and serve. He Himself was once a servant who washed the disciples' feet, served the masses and went away to the cross as the suffering servant to die for you. He was not ashamed to serve and die as a servant. Will you not want to be like Him? You can receive Him and He will come into your heart and make it possible for you to serve Him through serving man. If you receive Him and are a servant in this life, you will sit on the throne with Him in the other life and reign with Him. How wonderful!

9 If you refuse to receive Him, you will most likely fail as a servant now and possibly lose your job, continue in sin and on the Judgment Day, you will be thrown into the lake of fire to suffer for ever and ever as a servant of the devil. You would then have been a miserable servant in this life and a million times more miserable in the life to come.

10 You do well to receive the Lord Jesus. Do so now. Pray a prayer like the following one or make this one your own. "Lord Jesus, I am a sinner. Forgive me. Wash away my sin.

Come into my heart. Be my Lord and my God. I will obey You and manifest it in the way and in the same spirit with which I would serve You, were You physically present as my Master. I will not be an eye-servant or a man-pleaser. I want to serve You and believe that when You are satisfied, my earthly masters, too, will be satisfied. I promise to serve You from now on wherever I may be and whatever I may be doing. Thank You for receiving me as Yours and for coming into my heart and life. Amen."

A new day

A new day dawns in any home where the husband, wife, children and servants are committed to the total will of God, having each repented of their sin, received Jesus Christ and are consecrated to doing the will of God from their heart.

Has that new day dawned on your home or are you the obstacle to it because of your rebellion towards God, because of your love of sin? Will you be the first person in your family to open your heart to Jesus? Please do. God will then use you as a starting point from which to reach out to the others and save them. Act TODAY. God bless you!

CHAPTER 8

RELATIVES
AND
THE MARRIED LIFE

In 1971, I had the responsibility of listening to the story of a miserable woman, whose marriage had failed. She told me of some of the problems which she and her husband had had. Then she added, "Although we had these problems, our marriage would have survived and improved ; for we were getting to understand each other. What really ruined it was my brother. He insulted my husband continuously. He gave me orders and asked me to obey them. His orders were always to do something against my husband. I tried to obey him and sometimes I was confused and I did not know to whom I was to be loyal - my husband or my brother. When things failed, my brother blamed me for marrying the wrong man, but I know deep down in my heart that he is the one who ruined my marriage." There have been many complaints of a similar nature. Relatives have an impact on marriages, which can be positive or negative.

Remote control

Marriage is to be the union of one man and one woman, who separate themselves from all others to go on their own in life. When God the Author of marriage first decreed it, He said, *"Therefore a man leaves his father and mother and cleaves to his wife, and they become one flesh"* (Genesis 2:24). There must be a "leaving" before there is a "cleaving" and before there is a "one flesh." A man and a woman must first separate themselves from their family (father and mother) (leaving) and they must publicly testify to their commitment to each other (cleaving) and then and only then may they have the sexual and other union (one flesh). The leaving is often ignored and this leads to the ruin of many marriages. When I have conducted a wedding service, I have often asked the relatives of the couple that are present there to lift up their hands. Each one has been encouraged to lift up both hands as a sign that they are letting the couple go and will not try to control the marriage by various ways from a distance.

There are a number of things that are done which reduce the chances of a marriage from succeeding. We shall look at them very briefly and make comments.

1- THE WIFE IS MARRIED ON HIRE PURCHASE

Some people treat their daughters as cars on hire purchase. The only difference is that there is no fixed price for the car and further payment can be demanded at any time, depending on the financial needs of the seller. There are also so many people involved in the selling deal that it is impossible to tell who will be turning up when, for further demands of payment. When I was 21 years old and my parents had been married for thirty-four years, one of the relatives of my mother turned up at our home. I was greatly amused when my Daddy told me the reason for the visit. He had come to claim a part of his share of the bride price for my Mummy. He went away with our biggest cock and some money! I do not need to say that this is wickedness. It is exploitation. It must be condemned and stopped.

2 - EXCESSIVE FINANCIAL DEMANDS

I have known couples who have had to take a loan (and live poorly, with quarrels, due to insufficient funds to run the home because of the loan) in order to finance a development project in the wife's or husband's family. In one such case that I know of, there was such little money left that the angry husband once told the wife, "You are an instrument of bad-luck. I am going bankrupt because of you." He then put down his head and wept.

3 - REMOTE CONTROL OF HUSBAND AND/OR WIFE

There are those who feed their sons with ideas on how to get the wife under control, who suggest the need for a second wife if the baby is not coming quickly or who suggest and actually propose whom the second wife should be, because the first wife, being from a different tribe, does not cater for them as she should.

4 - MATERNAL STRINGS

There are those mothers who treat their married sons as if they were still the five year old kids that they had twenty or more years before. They worry about them and quarrel with their sons' wives as to how the food is cooked, when it is cooked and how it is served. They fuss around and point out all the weaknesses of their daughters-in-law to their sons, as if to say, "I am a better wife."

5 - THE HUMAN "SUITCASE"

Often when a girl is going into marriage, she is accompanied by a younger brother or sister, or any of those failing, a cousin or so. This accompaniment, who is like a human suitcase, is often too young to help in the house. The girl's relatives say that he is coming to help, but they really mean that they want some money from the husband by indirect taxation: the fees, the clothing, etc., of this human suitcase. So the couple has to start bringing up a big child before their first child has arrived.

6 - LONG AND EXTENDED VISITS

Sometimes, the husband's father (or mother or some other relative of his or the wife's) moves into the home and forgets that he has one of his own. He stays there for endless days, not only ungratefully enjoying the hospitality of the couple, but making dangerous comments that expose the faults of the member of the couple that is not from his side. This can only destroy a marriage.

Marriage is for two

In order to solve these problems, we state, first of all, that marriage is for two people: the husband and wife. It is not one family marrying another family. It is not 'the ten shall become one flesh;' but 'the two shall become one flesh'. This principle should be jealously guarded. The thought that the woman leaves to become a part of the husband's family so that his relatives call her "our wife" is totally foreign to the Author of marriage. God did not mean it to be so. He insists that the husband and wife must each leave before they cleave. The thought that a man should take his bride into one of the rooms of his parents' house is nonsense. If a man cannot provide a home away from his parents' house, he should not marry.

A - No man should accept to have a human suitcase accompanying his wife. The two people need some time together to grow to know each other and work out the principles on which they are to build their relationship and home. They must be allowed to do this without the interference of others.

B - The couple should refuse to have the marriage purchase deal. If they must pay, let them pay the bride price before marriage and refuse to have the continued exploitation by the girl's relatives. Daughters must take a firm stand with their parents against the traditions that make them expensive wares to be sold and the proceeds used to buy alcohol, cars and more women.

C - The husband must let his mother know that from the moment of his marriage, his primary loyalty has changed from her to his wife. From the point of marriage, the protocol in everything must be wife before mother. This lesson may be resisted violently, but it must be taught and insisted upon.

D - Financial gifts to relatives should be organised and given periodically so that no member of the family, be it the man's or the woman's, thinks that he can turn up any time and make money out of the couple. Such exploiters must be resisted firmly. The couple must, within the limits of their ability, provide for needy relatives. To live in luxury and turn a deaf ear to relatives in need is to go contrary to the instructions of God who is the Author of marriage. The financial needs of relatives of both husband and wife must be provided for and the determining factors should be

1. availability of funds

2. desperation of need

3. fairness to both families.

C - The financial responsibility of a man is first to his immediate family - his wife and children, and only secon-
darily and tertiarily to others. No one should feel obliged
to supply the financial needs of family members who are
able to work, have work to do, but prefer to be lazy. To
finance the needs of lazy people is to do evil. No man
should enter into debts. Debtors are sorrowful people. No
one should get into debts for others. If you do not have,
you cannot be expected by the Author of marriage to give
what you do not have.

F - Relatives should be encouraged to visit the couple, but
they should carry the following proverb on their hearts
and in their heads and live by it: *"Let your foot be seldom in
your neighbour's house, lest he be weary of you and hate you"*
(Proverbs 25:17). Husband and wife must be sensitive to
real needs. In a situation where a child has lost the parents,
it may be the right thing to take that child in and give him
a loving home. It could also be that some member of the
family is sick or recovering from an illness and needs care.
It could be that one of the parents is bereaved and ho-
meless at old age. It would only be loving and necessary
to take such into the home and show them abundant love
and care. Not to do this would be failing in love.

G - Relatives who stay in the house on visits like holidays, etc.,
should be incorporated into the work force of the house.

My two younger brothers have each spent a year with us (my parents are in heaven) before going to the University. Each one was made to serve as a servant in the house and not treated as a master. If visitors who stay for extended periods are made to work, they find their visit more interesting and their work will take away any feeling of exploitation. A proverb among my agricultural people says that he who has a right to the evening meal also has a duty to take up a hoe the next morning.

H - Relatives should be looked upon as human beings needing love and care. They should not just be looked upon as exploiters, even if that is their attitude. They are exploiting because they are bankrupt of love. Husbands and wives should show them love and so help to write off their bankruptcy.

I - The ultimate answer to the problems raised by relatives in the married life is a revolutionary encounter with the Lord Jesus. Many of these problems arise from man's estrangement from God. The human heart is filled with sin and self instead of with Christ and love. When a sinner turns from his sin and self and then receives Jesus Christ as his Lord and Saviour, his sins are taken away completely and the Lord Jesus comes in as Ruler and as Lord of that life. When the Lord Jesus comes in, the love of God is then shed abroad in the heart of such a person by the Holy Spirit. Such a person is then increasingly liberated from selfishness. He can love and he can accept love. When husband, wife and relatives each enter into this life-changing experience with Jesus, a new day dawns on the relationship; for their interactions will be in a spirit of loving and giving, instead of exploiting and demanding.

You can enter into that life-transforming experience with Jesus today. Do not wait for your wife or husband. Do not wait for your relatives. Turn to Jesus today. You can become the first in your family to turn to Him. He will then use you as an instrument to cause others to turn to Him. Is today not your Day? Will you not repent today? Why not now? Just now?

God bless you! Amen.

CHAPTER 9

STAYING IN LOVE
IN THE MARRIED LIFE

However badly a marriage may be going at the moment, however broken the relationship between the two people may be at the moment, some time in the past, the two people knew a happy moment or happy moments. There must have been a time when the two people entertained the idea that they could make it out together as husband and wife. Let each love story end up as it may, the beginning is always sweet. The trouble is that the sweet portion of the relationship may be over before the marriage begins, and the parties enter into the marriage because they do not want to hurt the other rather than because they are still enjoying the relationship.

Why do many relationships die?

I think there are a number of reasons. We shall briefly look at some of those and suggest remedies.

The first main reason is the fact that most relationships start outside the will of God. The parties involved have sinned and rebelled against God. They are living outside God's will and a relationship that was meant to satisfy, with God at the centre of the lives of the participants, fails because self is ruling the lives of one or both parties. So two sinners who continue in their sin will fail in their relationship.

The second reason is that the wrong parties are married to each other. A man whose shoe size is 9 will have a bad time with an excellent size 7 shoe. We have treated this theme exhaustively in Book Two: "Enjoying the Choice of Your Marriage Partner," and you should make sure that you read that book. It

will throw light on many areas of your life, whether you are engaged, married, divorced, hoping to be married or not hoping
ever to be married.

The third reason is that many people mistake emotional fe-
vers, which come on and off, for love and get married on the basis of these, and when the fever is over, they find that there was
no love on which to build the relationship.

The fourth reason is that the love is allowed to die. Love is,
in a sense, living. If well-nourished, it will grow and multiply. If
badly fed, it will become dwarfish. If starved or poisoned, it will
die from the starvation or poison. So to stay in love, the things
that poison love must be eliminated and the things that cause
love to grow must be brought in.

The following things poison and kill love :

1.   Harsh words.
2.   Cruel actions.
3.   Selfish attitudes.
4.   Excessive demands.
5.   Superficiality.
6.   Dishonesty.
7.   Lying.
8.   Marital unfaithfulness.
9.   Dirt and disorder.
10. Ugliness.
11. Gossip.
12. Coldness.

13. Foreign interference from relatives.
14. Spiritual backsliding.
15. Poor communication.
16. Separation from each other.
17. Pride.
18. Exposure of the faults of the partner to others.
19. Extravagance.
20. Lack of a clear sense of direction.
21. Poor leadership from the husband.
22. Insubmission from the wife.
23. Laziness.
24. Financial insecurity (the best security is that with God as the Guarantor).

The following cause love to grow:
1. Tender words.
2. Tender and understanding actions.
3. A selfless attitude.
4. Generosity.
5. Depth.
6. Honesty.
7. Truthfulness.
8. Faithfulness.
9. Cleanliness and order.
10. An attractive body.
11. Integrity.
12. Warmth.

13. Rejection of the interference of relatives.
14. Spiritual progress.
15. Good communication, openness.
16. Regular contact.
17. Convergent interests.
18. Humility.
19. Protection of the pride of the mate before others.
20. Responsible use of money and things.
21. A clear sense of direction.
22. Good leadership from the husband.
23. Submission from the wife.
24. Hard work from both parties.
25. Financial security.

The husband and wife should each ask themselves the following questions and do something about them. They should act quickly before their relationship reaches the point beyond which recovery is impossible.

1 -

    a. What was there in my physical appearance that first attracted my partner?

    b. Have I lost it?

    c. Can I regain it?

    d Is there anything in my appearance that shocks him/her?

2 -

    a.   What character traits did he/she like in me then?

    b.   Which ones have I lost?

    c.   What must I do to regain them?

3 -

    a.   What was my spiritual commitment then?

    b.   Have I backslidden or have I made too little   progress with time?

    c.   What must I do to be what he/she wants?

4 -

    a.   What things does he/she not want? Make a list of them.

    b.   Work out a program to eliminate them. They may include too much noise, dirt and disorder, etc.

5 -

    a.   What things does he/she want? Have I grown with his/her growing interests?

    b.   Make a list of them and work out a plan to introduce them into your life and that of the home.

    c.   Follow the plan seriously.

6 -   Is the attitude of my family to him/her building him/her or destroying? What can I do about it?

If you have lost the love of your partner, the fault is most probably yours. You have failed to maintain, develop, add that which is needed to keep his/her love. Why blame him/her? You did not feed the plant. You have starved or killed it. Wake up and do something about it while there is time. Instead of blaming your partner, see the fact that the fault is yours. If you take care of your part of it and look up to God, He will help your partner to take care of his or her own side of it.

You should do something about your relationship.

Start TODAY!

CHAPTER 10

MARRIED
IN HEAVEN

A young girl, very much in love with her fiancé once said to me, "Brother Zach, is there marriage in heaven?" I shall want to be married to John in heaven. I shall never ever want to be the wife of another."

Another young woman told a young man, " You are the one I ought to have married, but we met each other too late. Is there any chance that we could be married in heaven? It would be the fulfilment of all my dreams to be your wife in heaven."

I am sorry for these two. There will be marriage in heaven, but it will be marriage of another kind.

Jesus the heavenly husband

In heaven, Jesus will be the husband - the Bridegroom. The entire Bible talks of Him as the heavenly Bridegroom. John the Baptist, in talking about Jesus, said, *"No one can receive anything except what is given him from heaven. You yourselves bear me witness, that I said, I am not the Christ, but I have been sent before him. He who has the bride is the bridegroom ; the friend of the bridegroom, who stands and hears him, rejoices greatly at the bridegroom's voice ; therefore this joy of mine is now full. He must increase, but I must decrease"* (John 3:27-30). John testified to the fact that Jesus Christ is the heavenly Bridegroom.

Jesus often talked about the Kingdom of God as an invitation to a marriage supper. He is the Bridegroom.

John the apostle talks about the marriage of the Lamb of God. Jesus is the Lamb of God. When John the Baptist saw Him, he said, *"Behold, the Lamb of God, who takes away the sin of the world!"* (John 1:29). *" Let us rejoice and exult and give him the glory, for the marriage of the Lamb has come, and His Bride has made herself ready"* (Revelation 19:7).

Believers are the bride-to-be

Those who have turned from their sin, abandoned all their sinful ways and received Jesus Christ, become engaged to Jesus to become His bride on the wedding day. All who have received Jesus are so engaged to Him. The apostle Paul wrote to the Corinthian believers, *"I feel a divine jealousy for you, for I betrothed you to Christ to present you as a pure bride to her one husband. But I am afraid that as the serpent deceived Eve by his cunning, your thoughts will be led astray from a sincere and pure devotion to Christ"* (Il Corinthians II:2-3). Every true believer is really engaged to Christ. On the part of Christ, His commitment to the believer is so irrevocable that He considers her not only as His fiancée, but as His bride. He will never reject her. He will never change His mind about her, although He will not force her to Himself. The believer has the freedom to break the engagement.

All who have radically turned from their sin and turned to Christ make up the one Church of God. It does not matter the denomination to which they belong. All who have not turned from sin and turned to Christ do not belong to the Christ and do not belong to the Church of God. They belong to the church of Satan, regardless of their denomination. All who do the works of Satan, including :

cowardice

faithlessness

wickedness

murder

fornication

adultery

sorcery

idolatry

lying

etc,

belong to Satan and are members of the church of Satan. They are also engaged to Satan, to be his bride some day. Are you engaged to Jesus or to Satan? The one who rules your life is your fiancé. The one you obey is your husband-to-be.

All true believers, that is, the Church, are the bride-to-be of Christ. The Bible says, *"... Christ loved the Church and gave himself up for her, that he might sanctify her, having cleansed her by the washing of water with the word, that he might present the Church to himself in splendour, without blemish"* (Ephesians 5:25-27).

All who are real brides-to-be of Christ have the following characteristics :

1 They have accepted His death on the cross to purchase them.

2 They are sanctified by Christ.

3 They are cleansed by Christ.

4   They are increasingly being rendered by Christ without spot (sins) wrinkles (loss of first love for Him) and blemish (character faults).

The marriage will be in heaven

One day, not long from now, the trumpet of God will sound, *"And the dead in Christ will rise first; then we who are alive, who are left, shall be caught up together with them in the clouds to meet the Lord in the air, and so we shall always be with the Lord"* (1 Thessalonians 4:16-17).

When Jesus has come and taken His own to heaven, then the marriage will occur between Himself and His bride-to-be. After that, the bride-to-be will be His bride, His wife, for all eternity, and she will rule and reign with Him. The Bible says,

"'Hallelujah ! For the Lord our God the Almighty reigns. Let us rejoice and exult and give him the glory. For the marriage of the Lamb has come, and his bride has made herself ready; it was granted her to be clothed with fine linen, bright and pure - for the fine linen is the righteous deeds of the saints"* (Revelation 19:6-8).

The bride will dwell with the Lamb, the Bridegroom in the new Jerusalem. This new Jerusalem is called the Holy City. The Bible says, *"Then came one of the seven angels who had the seven bowls full of the seven last plagues, and spoke to me, saying, 'Come, I will show you the bride, the wife of the Lamb.* And in the Spirit he carried me away to a great, high mountain, and showed me the holy city Je-*

*rusalem coming down out of heaven from God, having the glory of God,
its radiance like a most rare jewel, like a jasper, clear as crystal"* (Revelation 21:9-11).

> *"And I saw the holy city, new Jerusalem, coming down out of heaven from God, prepared as a bride adorned for her husband ; and I heard a loud voice from the throne saying, 'Behold, the dwelling of God is with men. He will dwell with them, and they shall be his people, and God himself will be with them'"* (Revelation 21:2-3).

In the new Jerusalem, the Holy City, the Lord Jesus, the Heavenly Bridegroom will dwell with His bride, the Church, for ever and ever. The Church, each true believer, will enjoy the love of the Lord and live with Him in His immediate presence for ever and ever. It will be a most glorious marriage. It will fulfil all the desires and all the longings of the heart and being that cannot be fulfilled even in the best marriage on earth. Even if your earthly marriage is ruined and you are divorced, you can come to the Lord Jesus now. He will receive you and make you His bride-to-be for the heavenly marriage. Your marriage on earth may be an unending nightmare, an experience of hell on earth. If you do not repent, you will be in hell, married to Satan for ever and ever. But if you repent and receive Jesus, you can rejoice because He, who is your Heavenly Husband, is coming, and things will soon be wonderful.

I invite you to come to Christ, so that your earthly marriage is dramatically transformed through the power of Christ.

I invite you to come to Christ so that, regardless of the condition of your earthly life, you can rest in full assurance that you will be married to Christ throughout all eternity, and how wonderful it will be!

There in heaven, and married to Christ, the Bible says, *"He will wipe away every tear from their eyes, and death shall be no more, neither shall there be mourning nor crying nor pain any more, for the former things have passed away"* (Revelation 21:4).

Yes, it will be wonderful there, married to Christ.

There will be no marital unfaithfulness.

There will be no husbands who come back at 2 a.m.

There will be no husbands who beat, threaten and divorce.

There will be no dirty wives who make the home unbearable.

There will be no problem house-servants.

There will be no wicked neighbours.

There will be no accidents.

There will be Jesus.

And there will be Jesus.

Then there will be Jesus.

And, in addition, there will be Jesus.

And, to conclude it all, there will be Jesus.

You and Him.

He and you.

Both of You together.

For all eternity.

For ever and ever.

Won't you come to Him now?

God bless you!

Very Important

If you have not yet received Jesus as your Lord and Saviour, I encourage you to receive Him. Here are some steps to help you,

ADMIT that you are a sinner by nature and by practice and that on your own you are without hope. Tell God you have personally sinned against Him in your thoughts, words and deeds. Confess your sins to Him, one after another in a sincere prayer. Do not leave out any sins that you can remember. Truly turn from your sinful ways and abandon them. If you stole, steal no more. If you have been committing adultery or fornication, stop it. God will not forgive you if you have no desire to stop sinning in all areas of your life, but if you are sincere, He will give you the power to stop sinning.

BELIEVE that Jesus Christ, who is God's Son, is the only Way, the only Truth and the only Life. Jesus said, *"I am the way, the truth and the life; no one comes to the Father, but by me" (John 14:6). The Bible says, "For there is one God, and there is one mediator between God and men, the man Christ Jesus, who gave himself as a ransom for all" (1 Timothy 2:5-6). "And there is salvation in no one else (apart from Jesus), for there is no other name under heaven given among men by which we must be saved" (Acts 4:12). "But to all who received him, who believed in his name, he gave power to become children of God…"* (John 1:12). BUT,

CONSIDER the cost of following Him. Jesus said that all who follow Him must deny themselves, and this includes selfish financial, social and other interests. He also wants His followers to take up their crosses and follow Him. Are you prepared to abandon your own interests daily for those of Christ? Are you prepared to be led in a new direction by Him? Are you prepared to suffer for Him and die for Him if need be? Jesus will have nothing to do with half-hearted people. His demands are total. He will only receive and forgive those who are prepared to follow Him AT ANY COST.

Think about it and count the cost. If you are prepared to follow Him, come what may, then there is something to do:

INVITE Jesus to come into your heart and life. He says, "*Behold I stand at the door and knock. If anyone hears my voice and opens the door (to his heart and life), I will come in to him and eat with him, and he with me*" (Revelation 3:20). Why don't you pray a prayer like the following one or one of your own construction as the Holy Spirit leads?

> "Lord Jesus, I am a wretched, lost sinner who has sinned in thought, word and deed. Forgive all my sins and cleanse me. Receive me, Saviour and transform me into a child of God. Come into my heart now and give me eternal life right now. I will follow you at all costs, trusting the Holy Spirit to give me all the power I need."

When you pray this prayer sincerely, Jesus answers at once and justifies you before God and makes you His child.

Please write to me and I will pray for you and help you as you go on with Jesus Christ

***

If you have received the Lord Jesus-Christ after reading this book, please write to us at the following address:

For Europe:

Editions du Livre Chrétien
4, Rue du Révérend Père Cloarec
92400 Courbevoie
E-mail: editionlivrechretien@gmail.com

For Africa:

Christian Publishing House
P.O. Box 7100 Yaounde
Cameroon
E-mail: cphyaounde@yahoo.fr

ABOUT
THE AUTHOR

The author was born in the flesh on 20th June 1945 and born of the Holy Spirit on 13th June 1956. He made an absolute surrender of himself to the Lord Jesus and to His service on 01st October 1966, and was filled with the Holy Spirit on 24th October 1970.

The author was admitted to a first class in the Bachelor of Science degree and graduated as a prize winning student from Fourah Bay College in the University of Sierra Leone in October 1969. His research in Organic Chemistry led to the Ph.D., Doctor of Philosophy, awarded by the University of Makerere, Kampala in Uganda in October 1973. His published scientific work was recently evaluated by the University of Durham in Great Britain and found to be research of high distinction, for which he was awarded the D.Sc., Doctor of Science in October 2005. As a Professor of Organic Chemistry in the University of Yaounde I in Cameroon, the author has supervised or co-supervised 100 Master's Degree and Doctoral Degree theses and co-authored over 155 scientific articles in leading international journals. The author considers scientific research as an act of obedience to God's command to "subdue the earth" (Genesis 1:28). The author also knows that the Lord Jesus Christ is the Lord of Science. "For by him all things were created…" (Colossians 1:16). He made the Lord Jesus the Director of his research laboratory and he the author deputy director, and attributes his scientific success to the revelational leadership of the Lord Jesus.

The author has read over 1350 books on the Christian faith and has authored over 150 to advance the Gospel of Christ. Four million of his books are in circulation in eleven languages. Sixteen million Gospel tracts authored by him are in circulation in seventeen languages.

The author considers prayer to be the most important

work that can be done on earth for God and for man. He has over 50,000 recorded answers to prayer and is striving more and more to know God and to move Him to answer prayer. He and his team have carried out over 57 Prayer Crusades (a prayer crusade is a period of forty days and nights during which at least eight hours are invested into prayer each day). They have also carried out over 80 prayer sieges (a Prayer Siege is a time of near non-stop praying that ranges from 24 hours to 120 hours). He has carried out over 100 Prayer Walks of between five and forty-seven kilometres in towns and cities around the world. He has taught on prayer again and again, even though he is in many ways just a beginner in the profound science of prayer.

The author also considers fasting as one of the weapons for Christian Spiritual Warfare. He has carried out over 250 fasts ranging from three days to forty days, drinking water only or water and water soluble vitamins. Recently the author was called by the Lord to battle with the hosts of wickedness in heavenly places, was given a fasting body and asked to carry out supra long fasts of between 52 and 80 days. They are now being carried out.

The author, having seen something of the importance of redeeming money and investing it into the battle to reach those without Christ with the glorious Gospel, has chosen a life-style of simplicity and "self-imposed poverty" in order that their income should be invested into the critical work of evangelism, soul-winning, church-planting and the perfecting of the saints. He and his wife have grown to investing 92.5% of their earned income from all sources (salaries, allowances, royalties and cash gifts) into the Gospel with the hope that, as they grow in the knowledge and the love of the Lord and the perishing souls of people, they will one day invest 99% of their income into the Gospel.

In the last forty years, 99% of the time, the author has spent between 15 minutes and 06 hours daily with God alone in what he calls Daily Dynamic Encounters with God (DDEWG). During these times he has read God's Word, meditated on it, listened to God's voice, heard God speak to him, recorded what God was saying to him and prayed it through. He thus has over 18,000 recorded Daily Dynamic Encounters With God. He considers these daily meetings with God around His Word, the determinant strength of his life. These Daily Dynamic Encounters with God, coupled with over 60 periods of withdrawing to seek God alone for periods that ranged from 3 to 21 days (which he terms Retreats For Spiritual Progress), have slowly transformed the author into a man who first hungered for God, and now hungers and thirsts for God, while hoping to become a man who hungers, thirsts and gasps after God. "Oh that I would have more of God" is his unceasing inner cry.

The author has travelled extensively to preach the Gospel. He has gone out of his base in Yaounde on over 700 missionary journeys in Cameroon that range from one day to three weeks in duration, and on over 500 missionary journeys that range in duration from two days to six weeks to over 70 nations on all the six continents.

The author is the founding team-leader of Christian Missionary Fellowship International, an evangelism, soul-winning, church-planting and disciple making movement with missionaries and churches in over 50 nations on all the six continents.

The author and his team have seen over ten thousand recorded miracles of healing performed by the Lord in answer to prayer in Jesus' Name, ranging from the disappearance of headaches, to cancers disappearing, HIV positive people being transformed into HIV negative people; the blind seeing, the deaf hearing the dumb speaking, the lame walking, demoniacs set free, and new teeth and new organs received.

The author is married to Prisca and they have seven children who are involved with them in the Gospel. Prisca Zei Fomum is a national and international minister to children who specializes in winning children to the Lord Jesus and discipling them, imparting the vision of children's ministry, and the raising and building of ministers to children.

The author owes all that he is and all that the Lord has done in him and through him to the unmerited favours and blessings of the Lord God Almighty and to his worldwide army of friends and co-workers, who have generously and sacrificially invested their love, encouragement, fasts, prayers, gifts and co-operation into him, and their joint ministry. Without the unmerited favours and blessings of the Lord God Almighty and the investments of his friends and co-workers, he would have amounted to nothing.

13th March 2009

Cet ouvrage a été imprimé
en janvier 2014 par

FIRMIN-DIDOT

27650 Mesnil-sur-l'Estrée
N° d'impression : 121285
Dépôt légal : février 2014

Imprimé en France